William Shakespeare's
Julius Caesar
In Plain and Simple English

A SwipeSpeare™ Book

www.SwipeSpeare.com

Table of Contents

About This Series

The "SwipeSpeare™" series started as a way of telling Shakespeare for the modern reader—being careful to preserve the themes and integrity of the original. Visit our website SwipeSpeare.com to see other books in the series, as well as the interactive, and swipe-able, app!

The series is expanding every month. Visit BookCaps.com to see non-Shakespeare books in this series, and while you are there join the Facebook page, so you are first to know when a new book comes out.

Characters

Brutus-Supporter of the Republic and friend of Caesar

Julius Caesar-Roman general and senator

Antony-Loyal Friend of Caesar

Cassius-General

Octavius-Caesar's adopted son

Casca-A representative and one of the conspirators

Calpurnia-Caesar's wife

Portia-Brutus's wife and daughter of Cato

Flavius and Marullus-Two representatives

Cicero-Roman senator

Lepidus-Third member of Antony and Octavius's coalition

Decius-Member of the conspiracy

Comparative Version

Act I

Scene 1: Rome. A street.

Enter Flavius, Marullus and certain Commoners

Flavius
Hence! home, you idle creatures, get you home!
Is this a holiday? What! know you not,
Being mechanical, you ought not walk
Upon a laboring day without the sign
Of your profession?--Speak, what trade art thou?

Hey! Go home you lazy bums. Is this a holiday? What's going on? This is a work day. What is your occupation?

First Commoner
Why, sir, a carpenter.

I am a carpenter, sir.

Marullus
Where is thy leather apron and thy rule?
What dost thou with thy best apparel on?--
You, sir; what trade are you?

Where are your leather apron and your ruler? What are you doing in your best clothes? What is your occupation, sir?

Second Commoner
Truly, sir, in respect of a fine workman,
I am but, as you would say, a cobbler.

I am a cobbler, sir.

Marullus
But what trade art thou? Answer me directly.

But, what do you do? Answer me, honestly.

Second Commoner
A trade, sir, that, I hope, I may use with a safe
conscience, which is indeed, sir, a mender of
bad soles.

I mend bad soles, sir. That is my trade.

Marullus
What trade, thou knave?
Thou naughty knave, what trade?

That's not a trade, you liar. What kind of trade do you do?

Second Commoner

Nay, I beseech you, sir, be not out with me;
yet, if you be out, sir, I can mend you.

Please don't be angry, sir. I can show you.

Marullus
What mean'st thou by that?
Mend me, thou saucy fellow!

What do you mean? Show me?
Are you getting smart with me?

Second Commoner
Why, sir, cobble you.

I mean fix your shoes.

Flavius
Thou art a cobbler, art thou?

Oh, you are a shoe repairman.

Second Commoner
Truly, Sir, all that I live by is with the awl;
I meddle with no tradesman's matters, nor
women's matters, but with awl.
I am indeed, sir, a surgeon to old shoes;
when they are in great danger, I re-cover them.
As proper men as ever trod upon neat's-leather
have gone upon my handiwork.

Yes, sir. I live by the awl. I am not a political
man. I am like a doctor to old shoes.
I save their lives when they are in danger.
I have mended many a proper man's shoes.

Flavius
But wherefore art not in thy shop today?
Why dost thou lead these men about the streets?

Why are you not in your shop, today?
Why are you leading these men around?

Second Commoner
Truly, sir, to wear out their shoes to get myself
into more work. But indeed, sir, we make holiday
to see Caesar and to rejoice in his triumph.

I am hoping to get more work for myself by
wearing out their shoes. But, sir, we have
all taken off work to see Caesar and celebrate
his success.

Marullus
Wherefore rejoice? What conquest brings he
home? What tributaries follow him to Rome,
To grace in captive bonds his chariot wheels?
You blocks, you stones, you worse than senseless
things!
O you hard hearts, you cruel men of Rome,
Knew you not Pompey? Many a time and oft
Have you climb'd up to walls and battlements,
To towers and windows, yea, to chimney tops,
Your infants in your arms, and there have sat
The livelong day with patient expectation
To see great Pompey pass the streets of Rome.
And when you saw his chariot but appear,

What is he celebrating? What has he done
to receive such adoration? You idiots!
Once, you did whatever you could to cheer
on Pompey as he rode through the city of
Rome. Now, you put on your best clothes and
take off work to celebrate Pompey's murderer.
Go home and pray to the gods to keep the
plague away you deserve for such a showing
of ingratitude.

Have you not made an universal shout
That Tiber trembled underneath her banks
To hear the replication of your sounds
Made in her concave shores?
And do you now put on your best attire?
And do you now cull out a holiday?
And do you now strew flowers in his way
That comes in triumph over Pompey's blood?
Be gone! Run to your houses, fall upon your knees,
Pray to the gods to intermit the plague
That needs must light on this ingratitude.

Flavius

Go, go, good countrymen, and, for this fault,
Assemble all the poor men of your sort,
Draw them to Tiber banks, and weep your tears
Into the channel, till the lowest stream
Do kiss the most exalted shores of all.

Go on my fellow countrymen, and to make amends for your wrongdoings, go to the river Tiber and cry until its banks overflow.

Exit all the Commoners.

See whether their basest metal be not moved;
They vanish tongue-tied in their guiltiness.
Go you down that way towards the Capitol;
This way will I. Disrobe the images,
If you do find them deck'd with ceremonies.

Look at those morons leaving, speechless. Let's go down towards the Capitol and and take the decorations from the statues.

Marullus

May we do so?
You know it is the feast of Lupercal.

Can we do that? You know it is the feast of Lupercal.

Flavius

It is no matter; let no images
Be hung with Caesar's trophies. I'll about
And drive away the vulgar from the streets;
So do you too, where you perceive them thick.
These growing feathers pluck'd from Caesar's wing
Will make him fly an ordinary pitch,
Who else would soar above the view of men,
And keep us all in servile fearfulness.

It doesn't matter. I don't want any of the statues decorated for Caesar. Make sure you disperse any of the crowds. If we take away his supporters, maybe he will be more realistic and start treating us fairly, instead of using fear.

Exit.

Scene II: A public place.

Flourish. Enter Caesar. Antony, for the course. Calpurnia, Portia, Decius Brutus, Cicero, Brutus, Cassius, and Casca. A great crowd following, among them a soothsayer.

Caesar
Calpurnia,--

Calpurnia!

Casca
Peace, ho! Caesar speaks.

Be quiet, everyone! Caesar speaks.

Caesar
Calpurnia,--

Calpurnia!

Calpurnia
Here, my lord.

Here I am, my lord.

Caesar
Stand you directly in Antonius' way,
When he doth run his course.--Antonius,--

*You are standing in Antony's way
when he runs the race. Antony*

Antony
Caesar, my lord?

Yes, my lord?

Caesar
Forget not in your speed, Antonius,
To touch Calpurnia; for our elders say,
The barren, touched in this holy chase,
Shake off their sterile curse.

*Don't forget to touch Calpurnia when you
begin to race. The old men say if a childless
woman is touched in this holy race, she'll
become fertile.*

Antony
I shall remember.
When Caesar says "Do this," it is perform'd.

*I won't forget.
When you tell me to do something, it is as
good as done.*

Caesar
Set on; and leave no ceremony out.

*Okay, then. Get going, and don't leave out
any rituals.*

Flourish

Soothsayer
Caesar!

Caesar!

Caesar

Ha! Who calls?

Who's calling me?

Casca
Bid every noise be still.--Peace yet again!

Be quiet everyone!

Caesar
Who is it in the press that calls on me?
 I hear a tongue, shriller than all the music,
Cry "Caesar"! Speak, Caesar is turn'd to hear.

Who's calling me? I hear a shrill voice over the music crying, "Caesar!" Speak, I'm listening.

Soothsayer
Beware the Ides of March.

Beware the ides of March.

Caesar
What man is that?

Who is that?

Brutus
A soothsayer bids you beware the Ides of March.

A soothsayer is telling you to beware of March 15th.

Caesar
Set him before me; let me see his face.

Bring him to me. I want to see his face.

Cassius
Fellow, come from the throng; look upon Caesar.

Fellow, come out of the crowd. Look at Caesar.

Soothsayer approaches.

Caesar
What say'st thou to me now? Speak once again.

What do you want to say to me now? Speak again.

Soothsayer
Beware the Ides of March.

Beware of March 15th.

Caesar
He is a dreamer; let us leave him. Pass.

He's crazy. Let's leave.

Exit all except Brutus and Cassius.

Cassius
Will you go see the order of the course?

Are you going to watch the race?

Brutus
Not I

No, not me.

Cassius
I pray you, do.

Oh, please do.

Brutus

I am not gamesome; I do lack some part
Of that quick spirit that is in Antony.
Let me not hinder, Cassius, your desires;
I'll leave you.

I don't care for sports like Antony, but don't let me stop you, Cassius. I'll leave.

Cassius

Brutus, I do observe you now of late:
I have not from your eyes that gentleness
And show of love as I was wont to have:
You bear too stubborn and too strange a hand
Over your friend that loves you.

Brutus, I have observed lately that you don't seem to have the same feelings towards me, you once had. You have been stubborn and unfriendly to me, your friend who loves you.

Brutus

Cassius,
Be not deceived: if I have veil'd my look,
I turn the trouble of my countenance
Merely upon myself. Vexed I am
Of late with passions of some difference,
Conceptions only proper to myself,
Which give some soil perhaps to my behaviors;
But let not therefore my good friends be grieved—
Among which number, Cassius, be you one—
Nor construe any further my neglect,
Than that poor Brutus, with himself at war,
Forgets the shows of love to other men.

Cassius, don't be fooled. If I have looked differently lately, it has nothing to do with you. I have been preoccupied with personal affairs. So, don't worry about our relationship. Just know, that I am at war with myself and haven't been myself.

Cassius

Then, Brutus, I have much mistook your passion;
By means whereof this breast of mine hath buried
Thoughts of great value, worthy cogitations.
Tell me, good Brutus, can you see your face?

Well then, let me tell you I have been keeping some very interesting thoughts to myself. Brutus, can you see your face?

Brutus

No, Cassius, for the eye sees not itself
But by reflection, by some other thing.

No, Cassius, the eye cannot see itself, except in its reflection.

Cassius

'Tis just:
And it is very much lamented, Brutus,
That you have no such mirrors as will turn
Your hidden worthiness into your eye,
That you might see your shadow. I have heard
Where many of the best respect in Rome,--
Except immortal Caesar!-- speaking of Brutus,

True, but that's too bad. I wish you could see what others think about you. Many respect you almost as much as Caesar. They wish you could do something about the tyranny of today's government.

And groaning underneath this age's yoke,
Have wish'd that noble Brutus had his eyes.

Brutus
Into what dangers would you lead me, Cassius,
That you would have me seek into myself
For that which is not in me?

Cassius, to what are you alluding?
It sounds like something dangerous.
I don't have it in me.

Cassius
Therefore, good Brutus, be prepared to hear;
And since you know you cannot see yourself
So well as by reflection, I, your glass,
Will modestly discover to yourself
That of yourself which you yet know not of.
And be not jealous on me, gentle Brutus;
Were I a common laugher, or did use
To stale with ordinary oaths my love
To every new protester; if you know
That I do fawn on men, and hug them hard
And after scandal them; or if you know
That I profess myself, in banqueting,
To all the rout, then hold me dangerous.

Good Brutus, listen to what I have to say.
Let me be your mirror. If you don't believe me
to be genuine in my observations,
then consider me dangerous.

Flourish, and shouts.

Brutus
What means this shouting? I do fear the people
Choose Caesar for their king.

What does the shouting mean? I am afraid the
people choose Caesar for king.

Cassius
Ay, do you fear it?
Then must I think you would not have it so.

You fear it?
Then, I must believe you would have it
otherwise.

Brutus
I would not, Cassius; yet I love him well,
But wherefore do you hold me here so long?
What is it that you would impart to me?
If it be aught toward the general good,
Set honor in one eye and death i' the other
And I will look on both indifferently;
For let the gods so speed me as I love
The name of honor more than I fear death.

I wouldn't, Cassius. I love him very much.
So, what do you want to tell me?
What is so important? If it is good for
everyone, then I will listen even if it means
death. I love honor more than I fear death.

Cassius

I know that virtue to be in you, Brutus,
As well as I do know your outward favor.

I know you are honorable, Brutus.
I also know you are loyal to Caesar.

Well, honor is the subject of my story.
I cannot tell what you and other men
Think of this life; but, for my single self,
I had as lief not be as live to be
In awe of such a thing as I myself.
I was born free as Caesar; so were you:
We both have fed as well; and we can both
Endure the winter's cold as well as he:
For once, upon a raw and gusty day,
The troubled Tiber chafing with her shores,
Caesar said to me, "Darest thou, Cassius, now
Leap in with me into this angry flood
And swim to yonder point?" Upon the word,
Accoutred as I was, I plunged in,
And bade him follow: so indeed he did.
The torrent roar'd, and we did buffet it
With lusty sinews, throwing it aside
And stemming it with hearts of controversy;
But ere we could arrive the point proposed,
Caesar cried, "Help me, Cassius, or I sink!
I, as Aeneas, our great ancestor,
Did from the flames of Troy upon his shoulder
The old Anchises bear, so from the waves of Tiber
Did I the tired Caesar: and this man
Is now become a god; and Cassius is
A wretched creature, and must bend his body,
If Caesar carelessly but nod on him.
He had a fever when he was in Spain;
And when the fit was on him I did mark
How he did shake: 'tis true, this god did shake:
His coward lips did from their color fly;
And that same eye whose bend doth awe the world
Did lose his luster. I did hear him groan:
Ay, and that tongue of his that bade the Romans
Mark him, and write his speeches in their books,
Alas, it cried, "Give me some drink, Titinius,"
As a sick girl.--Ye gods, it doth amaze me,
A man of such a feeble temper should
So get the start of the majestic world,
And bear the palm alone.

Shout. Flourish.

Brutus
Another general shout!
I do believe that these applauses are

*But, my point is honor. I cannot speak for
other men, but for me, I cannot live
worshiping a man no more special than myself
Both Caesar and I were born free men.
We were friends, once, and I saved his life
in the river Tiber. I have also seen him cry out
like a sick little girl when we were in Spain.
Now, he is looked upon as if he was a god,
and I am a mere worker.*

*There's another shout. I believe they are for
Caesar.*

For some new honors that are heap'd on Caesar.

Cassius
Why, man, he doth bestride the narrow world
Like a Colossus; and we petty men
Walk under his huge legs and peep about
To find ourselves dishonorable graves.
Men at some time are masters of their fates:
The fault, dear Brutus, is not in our stars,
But in ourselves,that we are underlings.
"Brutus" and "Caesar": what should be in that
"Caesar"?
Why should that name be sounded more than
yours?
Write them together, yours is as fair a name;
Sound them, it doth become the mouth as well;
Weigh them, it is as heavy; conjure with them,
"Brutus" will start a spirit as soon as "Caesar."
Now, in the names of all the gods at once,
Upon what meat doth this our Caesar feed
That he is grown so great? Age, thou art shamed!
Rome, thou hast lost the breed of noble bloods!
When went there by an age since the great flood,
But it was famed with more than with one man?
When could they say, till now, that talk'd of Rome,
That her wide walls encompass'd but one man?
Now is it Rome indeed, and room enough,
When there is in it but one only man.
O, you and I have heard our fathers say
There was a Brutus once that would have brook'd
Th' eternal devil to keep his state in Rome,
As easily as a king!

He does walk around the world like a giant, while we petty men walk under his huge legs and look around until we are in our graves. Men may be the masters of their own fates but sometimes they do themselves an injustice. Why should Caesar be any more important than you? Your name is just as good as his. They are both easy to say. What makes him better than you? What has happened to Rome? Once, Rome bred many great men. Now, it seems there is only room for one. You know what our ancestors said. They would have let the devil rule Rome before a king.

Brutus
That you do love me, I am nothing jealous;
What you would work me to, I have some aim:
How I have thought of this, and of these times,
I shall recount hereafter; for this present,
I would not, so with love I might entreat you,
Be any further moved. What you have said,
I will consider; what you have to say,
I will with patience hear; and find a time
Both meet to hear and answer such high things.
Till then, my noble friend, chew upon this:
Brutus had rather be a villager
Than to repute himself a son of Rome

I know you love me, but I am not jealous. I think I know what you want me to do. I have thought of this before, but for now, I ask that you say no more. Listen to me. I had rather be a nobody than a Roman living in these conditions.

Under these hard conditions as this time
Is like to lay upon us.

Cassius
I am glad that my weak words
Have struck but thus much show of fire from
Brutus.

I am glad my simple words have moved you.

Brutus
The games are done, and Caesar is returning.

The race is over and Caesar is coming back.

Cassius
As they pass by, pluck Casca by the sleeve;
And he will, after his sour fashion, tell you
What hath proceeded worthy note today.

As the crowd passes by, get Casca's attention.
He will tell you what happened today.

Re-enter Caesar and his Train.

Brutus
I will do so.--But, look you, Cassius,
The angry spot doth glow on Caesar's brow,
And all the rest look like a chidden train:
Calpurnia's cheek is pale; and Cicero
Looks with such ferret and such fiery eyes
As we have seen him in the Capitol,
Being cross'd in conference by some senators.

I will, but look, Cassius. Caesar looks angry
and the rest look like a broken train.
Calpurnia looks pale and Cicero looks angry,
like he does in the Capitol when senators
disagree with him.

Cassius
Casca will tell us what the matter is.

Casca will tell us what's going on.

Caesar
Antonius,--

Antony!

Antony
Caesar?

Caesar?

Caesar
Let me have men about me that are fat;
Sleek-headed men, and such as sleep o' nights:
Yond Cassius has a lean and hungry look;
He thinks too much: such men are dangerous.

Surround me with fat, lazy men. See Cassius
over there. He has a hungry look about him,
and he thinks too much. Men, like him,
are dangerous.

Antony
Fear him not, Caesar; he's not dangerous;
He is a noble Roman and well given.

You needn't fear him. He's not dangerous.
He is a well-known and noble Roman.

Caesar

Would he were fatter! But I fear him not:
Yet, if my name were liable to fear,
I do not know the man I should avoid
So soon as that spare Cassius. He reads much;
He is a great observer, and he looks
Quite through the deeds of men: he loves no plays,
As thou dost, Antony; he hears no music:
Seldom he smiles; and smiles in such a sort
As if he mock'd himself and scorn'd his spirit
That could be moved to smile at any thing.
Such men as he be never at heart's ease
Whiles they behold a greater than themselves;
And therefore are they very dangerous.
I rather tell thee what is to be fear'd
Than what I fear, for always I am Caesar.
Come on my right hand, for this ear is deaf,
And tell me truly what thou think'st of him.

I don't fear him, but I wish he were fatter! Cassius, if I were fearful, is the kind of man one should fear. He is well-read and watches everything closely. He has no joys, like plays or music. He rarely smiles, and if he does it's at something he said. Men, like Cassius, are never at ease, especially around someone greater than themselves. Therefore, they are dangerous. I am just telling you what should be feared; not what I fear, for I am Caesar. Now, come on my right side, because my left ear is deaf and tell me what you think of him.

Trumpets play. Caesar exits with all his followers except Casca.

Casca

You pull'd me by the cloak;
would you speak with me?

You tugged on my sleeve. Do you want to speak with me?

Brutus

Ay, Casca, tell us what hath chanced today,
That Caesar looks so sad.

Yes, Casca. Tell us what happened today that made Caesar look so sad.

Casca

Why, you were with him, were you not?

Why? Weren't you with him?

Brutus

I should not then ask Casca what had chanced.

I wouldn't have asked if I were.

Casca

Why, there was a crown offer'd him;
and being offer'd him, he put it by with the back
of his hand, thus; and then the people fell
a-shouting.

Someone offered him a crown and he pushed it aside with the back of his hand, like this. Then, the people started shouting.

Brutus

What was the second noise for?

What was the second shout for?

Casca

Why, for that too.

Same thing.

Cassius
They shouted thrice: what was the last cry for?

They shouted three times. What was the last cry for?

Casca
Why, for that too.

Same reason as the first two.

Brutus
Was the crown offer'd him thrice?

Was the crown offered to him three times?

Casca
Ay, marry, was't, and he put it by thrice,
every time gentler than other; and at every
putting-by mine honest neighbors shouted.

Yes and each time he turned it down gently, and the crowds started shouting.

Cassius
Who offer'd him the crown?

Who offered him the crown?

Casca
Why, Antony.

Antony.

Brutus
Tell us the manner of it, gentle Casca.

Tell us how it happened.

Casca
I can as well be hang'd, as tell the manner of it:
it was mere foolery; I did not mark it.
I saw Mark Antony offer him a crown;--yet
'twas not a crown neither, 'twas one of these
coronets;--and, as I told you, he put it by once:
but, for all that, to my thinking, he would fain
have had it. Then he offered it to him again:
then he put it by again: but, to my thinking,
he was very loath to lay his fingers off it.
And then he offered it the third time; he put it
the third time by; and still, as he refused it,
the rabblement shouted, and clapp'd their chopt
hands, and threw up their sweaty night-caps,
and uttered such a deal of stinking breath
because Caesar refused the crown, that it had
almost choked Caesar, for he swooned and
fell down at it: and for mine own part, I durst
not laugh for fear of opening my lips and
receiving the bad air.

I just as soon be hanged as to tell it, it was so foolish. I didn't pay much attention. I saw Mark Antony offer him a crown. It was really just one of those head pieces. Anyway, Caesar turned it down, although I thought he wanted it. Then, Antony offered it to him again, and he pushed it away, but this time his hand stayed on it longer. Then, the third time Antony offered it the crowd went wild throwing up their sweaty hats and yelling that Caesar passed out. As for myself, I didn't dare laugh, for fear of breathing in the stench.

Cassius
But, soft! I pray you. What, did Caesar swoon?

Tell us again. Did you say Caesar fainted?

Casca
He fell down in the market-place, and foam'd at mouth, and was speechless.

He fell down in the market-place and began foaming at the mouth. He couldn't even speak.

Brutus
'Tis very like: he hath the falling-sickness.

Sounds like he has the falling sickness.

Cassius
No, Caesar hath it not; but you, and I,
And honest Casca, we have the falling-sickness.

No, Caesar doesn't have it, but we do.

Casca
I know not what you mean by that; but I am sure Caesar fell down. If the tag-rag people did not clap him and hiss him, according as he pleased and displeased them, as they use to do the players in the theatre, I am no true man.

I don't know what you mean, but I am telling the truth. The crowd responded to him in pleasure and displeasure, just like they do in the theater.

Brutus
What said he when he came unto himself?

What did he say when he came around?

Casca
Marry, before he fell down, when he perceived the common herd was glad he refused the crown, he pluck'd me ope his doublet, and offered them his throat to cut: an I had been a man of any occupation, if I would not have taken him at a word, I would I might go to hell among the rogues:--and so he fell. When he came to himself again, he said, if he had done or said any thing amiss, he desired their worships to think it was his infirmity. Three or four wenches where I stood cried, "Alas, good soul!" and forgave him with all their hearts. But there's no heed to be taken of them: if Caesar had stabb'd their mothers, they would have done no less.

Before he fell, he opened up his robe and offer them his throat to cut. If I were a different man I might go to hell with that offer. Then, he fainted. When he came back around, he said it was just his illness. Three or four women by me cried, "Ah, poor soul!" But, they would have done that if Caesar had just stabbed their mothers.

Brutus
And, after that he came, thus sad away?

And after that, he came back looking so sad?

Casca
Ay.

Yes.

Cassius
Did Cicero say any thing?

Did Cicero say anything?

Casca
Ay, he spoke Greek.

Yes, he spoke in Greek.

Cassius
To what effect?

What did he say?

Casca
Nay, an I tell you that, I'll ne'er look you i' the face again: but those that understood him smiled at one another and shook their heads; but for mine own part, it was Greek to me. I could tell you more news too: Marullus and Flavius, for pulling scarfs off Caesar's images, are put to silence. Fare you well. There was more foolery yet, if could remember it.

I don't know. It was all Greek to me, but I can tell you those who understood him were smiling and shaking their heads. Also, Marullus and Flavius were punished for taking the decorations off the statues of Caesar. There was some more foolishness, but I can't remember.

Cassius
Will you sup with me tonight, Casca?

Will you have dinner with me tonight, Casca?

Casca
No, I am promised forth.

No, I already have plans.

Cassius
Will you dine with me tomorrow?

How about tomorrow night?

Casca
Ay, if I be alive, and your mind hold, and your dinner worth the eating.

Yes, if I'm alive and you still will have me and of course if the food's any good.

Cassius
Good; I will expect you.

Good, I'll be expecting you.

Casca
Do so; farewell both.

You do that. Goodbye, fellows.

Exit

Brutus
What a blunt fellow is this grown to be!
He was quick mettle when he went to school.

What a forward guy he has become!
He was always so shy in school.

Cassius
So is he now in execution
Of any bold or noble enterprise,

He's smart though, even if he plays stupid.
He comes across as abrasive, but it's just a

However he puts on this tardy form.
This rudeness is a sauce to his good wit,
Which gives men stomach to digest his words
With better appetite.

Brutus
And so it is. For this time I will leave you:
Tomorrow, if you please to speak with me,
I will come home to you; or, if you will,
Come home to me, and I will wait for you.

Cassius
I will do so: till then, think of the world.--

Exit Brutus.

Well, Brutus, thou art noble; yet, I see,
Thy honorable metal may be wrought,
From that it is disposed: therefore 'tis meet
That noble minds keep ever with their likes;
For who so firm that cannot be seduced?
Caesar doth bear me hard, but he loves Brutus;
If I were Brutus now and he were Cassius,
He should not humor me. I will this night,
In several hands, in at his windows throw,
As if they came from several citizens,
Writings all tending to the great opinion
That Rome holds of his name; wherein obscurely
Caesar's ambition shall be glanced at:
And after this let Caesar seat him sure;
For we will shake him, or worse days endure.

Exit.

way to get people to listen to him.

*You're probably right. I've got to go, though.
If you want to talk tomorrow, you can come to
my house, or I will go to yours.*

Sounds good. Till then, think about the world.

*Well, Brutus, you are noble, but not so noble
that you can't be swayed. That's why we must
stick together. Caesar may not like me, but he
loves Brutus. Now, if I was Brutus and he
was me, he wouldn't have listened to me
tonight. So, I will write several letters in
different handwriting to disguise their true
sender to convey the feelings of Rome;
Brutus is loved and Caesar is too ambitious.
After that, let's see how long Caesar keeps
his throne or worse.*

Scene III: The same. A street.

Thunder and lightning. Enter Casca with his sword drawn opposite of Cicero.

Cicero

Good even, Casca: brought you Caesar home?

Why are you breathless, and why stare you so?

Good evening, Casca. Are you coming from Caesar's house?
Caesar's house? Why are you breathless and bewildered?

Casca

Are not you moved, when all the sway of earth
Shakes like a thing unfirm? O Cicero,
I have seen tempests, when the scolding winds
Have rived the knotty oaks; and I have seen
Th' ambitious ocean swell and rage and foam,
To be exalted with the threatening clouds:
But never till tonight, never till now,
Did I go through a tempest dropping fire.
Either there is a civil strife in heaven,
Or else the world too saucy with the gods,
Incenses them to send destruction.

Aren't you moved when all of the earth is shaking? Oh Cicero, I have seen storms when the winds broke old oak trees and I have seen the ocean swell and rage with foam, but I have never seen a storm that dropped fire like rain. Not until tonight, not until now. Either there is a storm in heaven or the world is about to come to an end.

Cicero

Why, saw you anything more wonderful?

What have you seen so strange?

Casca

A common slave--you'd know him well by sight—
Held up his left hand, which did flame and burn
Like twenty torches join'd, and yet his hand
Not sensible of fire remain'd unscorch'd.
Besides,--I ha' not since put up my sword,--
Against the Capitol I met a lion,
Who glared upon me, and went surly by,
Without annoying me: and there were drawn
Upon a heap a hundred ghastly women,
Transformed with their fear; who swore they saw
Men, all in fire, walk up and down the streets.
And yesterday the bird of night did sit
Even at noonday upon the marketplace,
Howling and shrieking. When these prodigies
Do so conjointly meet, let not men say
"These are their reasons; they are natural";
For I believe they are portentous things

I saw a familiar slave hold up his hand. It was on fire, but it didn't get burned. Then, when I took out my sword, I saw a lion that looked at me but didn't attack. Later, there were a hundred women who swore they saw men on fire walking down the streets. Yesterday, the night owl was I the marketplace hooting at noon. When these things take place, we must pay attention. They are an omen of bad things to come.

Unto the climate that they point upon.

Cicero
Indeed, it is a strange-disposed time.
But men may construe things after their fashion,
Clean from the purpose of the things themselves.
Comes Caesar to the Capitol tomorrow?

That is certainly strange, but men sometimes see things they want to see that aren't actually correct. Is Caesar coming to the Capitol tomorrow?

Casca
He doth, for he did bid Antonius
Send word to you he would be there to-morrow.

He is because he told Antony to tell you he would be there tomorrow.

Cicero
Good then, Casca: this disturbed sky
Is not to walk in.

Good night then, Cicero. This is not a good night to walk around according to the sky.

Exit Cicero.

Enter Cassius.

Cassius
Who's there?

Who's there?

Casca
A Roman.

A Roman.

Cassius
Casca, by your voice.

I recognize your voice, Casca.

Casca
Your ear is good. Cassius, what night is this!

You've got a good ear, Cassius! What a night this has been!

Cassius
A very pleasing night to honest men.

It has been a good night for honest men.

Casca
Who ever knew the heavens menace so?

Who knew the heavens could be so menacing?

Cassius
Those that have known the earth so full of faults.
For my part, I have walk'd about the streets,
Submitting me unto the perilous night;
And, thus unbraced, Casca, as you see,
Have bared my bosom to the thunder-stone;
And when the cross blue lightning seem'd to open
The breast of heaven, I did present myself

Those that have known the earth's faults, like me. I walked about the streets welcoming the thunder and the lightning.

Even in the aim and very flash of it.

Casca
But wherefore did you so much tempt the Heavens? *Why would you tempt the heavens like that?*
It is the part of men to fear and tremble, *Most men would tremble with fear when the*
When the most mighty gods by tokens send *gods send us such astonishing sights.*
Such dreadful heralds to astonish us.

Cassius
You are dull, Casca;and those sparks of life *You are dumb, Casca. You lack the*
That should be in a Roman you do want, *characteristics of a Roman, or else you aren't*
Or else you use not. You look pale and gaze, *showing them. If you think about all of these*
And put on fear and cast yourself in wonder, *strange occurrences, you would realize,*
 To see the strange impatience of the Heavens: *it's the gods foreshadowing some awful things*
But if you would consider the true cause *to come. Right now, I can think of an ordinary*
Why all these fires, why all these gliding ghosts, *man in the Capitol who, like these strange*
Why birds and beasts,from quality and kind; *occurrences, performs unbelievable acts.*
Why old men, fools, and children calculate;--
Why all these things change from their ordinance,
Their natures, and preformed faculties
To monstrous quality;--why, you shall find
That Heaven hath infused them with these spirits,
To make them instruments of fear and warning
Unto some monstrous state. Now could I,
Casca,
Name to thee a man most like this dreadful night;
That thunders, lightens, opens graves, and roars,
As doth the lion in the Capitol;
A man no mightier than thyself or me
In personal action; yet prodigious grown,
And fearful, as these strange eruptions are.

Casca
'Tis Caesar that you mean; is it not, Cassius? *You're talking about Caesar, aren't you,*
Cassius?

Cassius
Let it be who it is: for Romans now *Whoever. We may look like our Roman*
Have thews and limbs like to their ancestors; *forefathers, but we are acting like our*
But, woe the while! our fathers' minds are dead, *mothers.*
And we are govern'd with our mothers' spirits;
Our yoke and sufferance show us womanish.

Casca
Indeed they say the senators to-morrow *True. They say the senators are planning on*
Mean to establish Caesar as a king; *making Caesar king, tomorrow. He will wear*
And he shall wear his crown by sea and land, *his crown everywhere, except here in Italy.*

In every place save here in Italy.

Cassius
I know where I will wear this dagger then;
Cassius from bondage will deliver Cassius:
Therein, ye gods, you make the weak most strong;
Therein, ye gods, you tyrants do defeat:
Nor stony tower, nor walls of beaten brass,
Nor airless dungeon, nor strong links of iron
Can be retentive to the strength of spirit;
But life, being weary of these worldly bars,
Never lacks power to dismiss itself.
If I know this, know all the world besides,
That part of tyranny that I do bear
I can shake off at pleasure.

I know where this dagger will be worn, then.
I will not be reined. Nothing can deter me,
not even death. Let everyone know that I can
shake off the threat of tyranny, when I want.

Thunder continues.

Casca
So can I:
So every bondman in his own hand bears
The power to cancel his captivity.

So can I.
Every man has the strength to overcome
bondage.

Cassius
And why should Caesar be a tyrant then?
Poor man! I know he would not be a wolf,
But that he sees the Romans are but sheep:
He were no lion, were not Romans hinds.
Those that with haste will make a mighty fire
Begin it with weak straws: what trash is Rome,
What rubbish, and what offal, when it serves
For the base matter to illuminate
So vile a thing as Caesar! But, O grief,
Where hast thou led me? I perhaps speak this
Before a willing bondman: then I know
My answer must be made; but I am arm'd,
And dangers are to me indifferent.

Poor Caesar! He thinks Romans are sheep
and he is a wolf. He wouldn't be a lion,
if Rome weren't acting like a bunch of
donkeys. People, who want to make a big fire,
start with little sticks. Rome has become
complete trash, the way it adores Caesar.
But, wait, I may be talking to someone who
wants to be a slave. Then, I may be in danger
for what I'm saying. It doesn't matter because
I am armed and not afraid.

Casca
You speak to Casca; and to such a man
That is no fleering tell-tale. Hold, my hand:
Be factious for redress of all these griefs;
And I will set this foot of mine as far
As who goes farthest.

Hey, you're talking to me. I'm not two-faced.
I won't tell anyone. Let's shake and join
together to right these wrongs.
I will go as far as any man.

Cassius

There's a bargain made.
Now know you, Casca, I have moved already
Some certain of the noblest-minded Romans
To undergo with me an enterprise
Of honorable-dangerous consequence;
And I do know by this, they stay for me
In Pompey's Porch: for now, this fearful night,
There is no stir or walking in the streets;
And the complexion of the element
Is favor'd like the work we have in hand,
Most bloody, fiery, and most terrible.

That's a deal. Now, I must tell you, I have already been working on some of the noblest minds in Rome to join with me in overthrowing Caesar. But, it's going to be dangerous, so we are meeting tonight at Pompey's porch because no one will be out in this weather.

Casca
Stand close awhile, for here comes one in haste.

Hang on. Here comes someone now.

Cassius
'Tis Cinna; I do know him by his gait;
He is a friend.--

It's Cinna. I recognize his walk. He is a friend.

Enter Cinna

Cinna, where haste you so?

Cinna, where are you going in such a hurry?

Cinna
To find out you. Who's that? Metellus Cimber?

To find you. Who's that? Metellus Cimber?

Cassius
No, it is Casca, one incorporate
To our attempts. Am I not stay'd for, Cinna?

No, it's Casca. He is one of us. Are the others ready?

Cinna
I am glad on't. What a fearful night is this! *Good, I'm glad. This has been a scary night.*
There's two or three of us have seen strange sights. *There are a couple of guys who have seen some strange sights.*

Cassius
Am I not stay'd for? tell me.

Have the people gathered? Tell me.

Cinna
Yes, You are. O Cassius, if you could but win
The noble Brutus to our party,--

Yes, they are. Please bring Brutus to join us.

Cassius
Be you content. Good Cinna, take this paper,
And look you lay it in the praetor's chair,
Where Brutus may but find it; and throw this
In at his window; set this up with wax

Be patient, good Cinna. Take this paper and put it in the chair where Brutus sits, throw this in his window, and put this on old Brutus's statue. When you have done all this,

Upon old Brutus' statue: all this done,
Repair to Pompey's Porch, where you shall find us.
Is Decius Brutus and Trebonius there?

go to the theater where we will be.
Are Decius Brutus and Trebonius there?

Cinna
All but Metellus Cimber, and he's gone
To seek you at your house. Well, I will hie
And so bestow these papers as you bade me.

Everyone is there but Metellus Cimber.
He's gone to your house looking for you.
Well, I'll go deliver these papers as you wish.

Cassius
That done, repair to Pompey's theatre.--

When you're done, go to Pompey's theater.

Exit Cinna.

Come, Casca, you and I will yet, ere day,
See Brutus at his house: three parts of him
Is ours already; and the man entire,
Upon the next encounter, yields him ours.

Come on, Casca. You and I will go to Brutus's
house. He is three-fourths ours, and I bet after
our visit we will have him completely.

Casca
O, he sits high in all the people's hearts!
And that which would appear offense in us,
His countenance, like richest alchemy,
Will change to virtue and to worthiness.

The people love him. So, with him we can do
no wrong in their eyes.

Cassius
Him, and his worth, and our great need of him,
You have right well conceited. Let us go,
For it is after midnight; and, ere day,
We will awake him, and be sure of him.
Exit.

You are so right. We need him.
Let's go for it's almost midnight
We will wake him up.

Act II

Scene I: Rome. Brutus's orchard.

Enter Brutus.

Brutus
What, Lucius, ho!--
I cannot, by the progress of the stars,
Give guess how near to day.--Lucius, I say!--
I would it were my fault to sleep so soundly.--
When, Lucius, when! Awake, I say! What, Lucius!

What's going on, Lucius?
What time is it? I say, Lucius!
I can't believe I slept so soundly.
Wake up, Lucius! What time is it? Lucius!

Enter Lucius

Lucius
Call'd you, my lord?

Did you call, my lord?

Brutus
Get me a taper in my study, Lucius:
When it is lighted, come and call me here.

Bring a candle to my study, Lucius,
and when it is lit, call me.

Lucius
I will, my lord.

I will, my lord.

Exit.

Brutus
It must be by his death: and, for my part,
I know no personal cause to spurn at him,
But for the general. He would be crown'd:
How that might change his nature,
there's the question:
It is the bright day that brings forth the adder;
And that craves wary walking. Crown him?--that:
And then, I grant, we put a sting in him,
That at his will he may do danger with.
Th' abuse of greatness is, when it disjoins

If Caesar wants to be crowned, despite what
may happen, what part do I play? I have no
reason to want his death, but Rome's best
interest is at hand. I wonder if it will change
his nature. Everyone knows that when one
climbs the ladder of success and reaches the
top rung, the climber's back is turned on
everyone below him. Caesar may become
high-minded and power-hungry. If so,
his life must be taken.

Remorse from power; and, to speak truth of
Caesar,
I have not known when his affections sway'd
More than his reason. But 'tis a common proof,
That lowliness is young ambition's ladder,
Whereto the climber-upward turns his face;
But, when he once attains the upmost round,
He then unto the ladder turns his back,
Looks in the clouds, scorning the base degrees
By which he did ascend: so Caesar may;
Then, lest he may, prevent. And, since the quarrel
Will bear no color for the thing he is,
Fashion it thus,--that what he is, augmented,
Would run to these and these extremities:
And therefore think him as a serpent's egg
Which hatch'd, would, as his kind grow mischievous;
And kill him in the shell.

Re-enter Lucius.

Lucius
The taper burneth in your closet, sir.
Searching the window for a flint I found
This paper thus seal'd up, and I am sure
It did not lie there when I went to bed.

*The candle is lit in your study, sir.
While I was looking for the flint, I found this
sealed letter. I'm sure it wasn't there earlier.*

Brutus
Get you to bed again; it is not day.
Is not tomorrow, boy, the Ides of March?

*Go to bed, now. Isn't tomorrow the Ides of
March?*

Lucius
I know not, sir.

I don't know, sir.

Brutus
Look in the calendar, and bring me word.

Look in the calendar, and let me know.

Lucius
I will, sir.

I will, sir.

Exit.

Brutus
The exhalations, whizzing in the air

The sky is lit by stars and meteors so,

Give so much light that I may read by them.—
[Opens the letter and reads.]

*I may read this letter.
Opens the letter and reads.*

"Brutus, thou sleep'st: awake and see thyself.
Shall Rome, &c. Speak, strike, redress--!
Brutus, thou sleep'st: awake!--"
Such instigations have been often dropp'd
Where I have took them up.
"Shall Rome, & c." Thus must I piece it out:
Shall Rome stand under one man's awe?
What, Rome?
My ancestors did from the streets of Rome
The Tarquin drive, when he was call'd a king.--
"Speak, strike, redress!"--Am I entreated, then,
To speak and strike? O Rome, I make thee promise,
If the redress will follow, thou receivest
Thy full petition at the hand of Brutus!

"Brutus, You are asleep. Wake up and see what is happening to Rome. Speak, strike, help us! Brutus, you are asleep. Wake up and take action. What is going to happen to Rome Should it be ruled by one man? Our ancestors drove off King Tarquin. Speak, strike, help!" Am I supposed to speak and strike. Oh, Rome, I promise you I will help protect you.

Re-enter Lucius.

Lucius
Sir, March is wasted fifteen days.

Tomorrow is March fourteenth.

Knocking within.

Brutus
'Tis good. Go to the gate, somebody knocks.--

Good. Go the gate and see who is knocking.

Exit Lucius.

Since Cassius first did whet me against Caesar
I have not slept.
Between the acting of a dreadful thing
And the first motion, all the interim is
Like a phantasma or a hideous dream:
The genius and the mortal instruments
Are then in council; and the state of man,
Like to a little kingdom, suffers then
The nature of an insurrection.

Since Cassius first told me he wants me to go against Caesar, I haven't slept. My mind has been filled with thought of taking action against the General. My body and my mind are in turmoil.

Re-enter Lucius.

Lucius
Sir, 'tis your brother Cassius at the door,
Who doth desire to see you.

Sir, it's your brother, Cassius, at the door. He wants to see you.

Brutus
Is he alone?

Is he by himself?

Lucius
No, sir, there are more with him.

No, sir. More men are with him.

Brutus
Do you know them?

Do you know any of them?

Lucius
No, sir, their hats are pluck'd about their ears,
And half their faces buried in their cloaks,
That by no means I may discover them
By any mark of favor.

I can't see their faces because their hats are pulled down and their faces are half buried in their coats.

Brutus
Let 'em enter.--

Let them come in.

Exit Lucius.

They are the faction.--O conspiracy,
Shamest thou to show thy dangerous brow by night,
When evils are most free? O, then, by day
Where wilt thou find a cavern dark enough
To mask thy monstrous visage?
Seek none, conspiracy;
Hide it in smiles and affability:
For if thou pass, thy native semblance on,
Not Erebus itself were dim enough
To hide thee from prevention.

They are the conspirators. Only dangerous activities take place by night, when evil is most free. In the day, how will they continue to hide their plans. If they showed their true plans, hell would not be able to hide them from being found.

Enter the conspirators, Cassius, Casca, Decius Brutus, Cinna, Metellus Cimber, and Trebonius.

Cassius
I think we are too bold upon your rest:
Good morrow, Brutus; do we trouble you?

Are we bothering you, Brutus? We are probably disturbing your rest. Good night.

Brutus
I have been up this hour, awake all night.
Know I these men that come along with you?

I have been up and awake all night. Do I know your companions?

Cassius
Yes, every man of them; and no man here
But honors you; and every one doth wish
You had but that opinion of yourself
Which every noble Roman bears of you.
This is Trebonius.

Yes, you know everyone. All of the men think very highly of you. This is Trebonius.

Brutus

He is welcome hither.

He is welcome here.

Cassius

This Decius Brutus.

This is Decius Brutus.

Brutus

He is welcome too.

He is also welcome.

Cassius

This, Casca; this, Cinna; and this, Metellus
Cimber.

This is Casca, Cinna, and Metellus Cimber.

Brutus

They are all welcome.--
What watchful cares do interpose themselves
Betwixt your eyes and night?

They are all welcome.
What brings you here this time of night?

Cassius

Shall I entreat a word?

I was hoping to have a word with you.

Brutus and Cassius whisper.

Decius Brutus

Here lies the east: doth not the day break here?

This is the east. Doesn't the sun rise here?

Casca

No.

No.

Cinna

O, pardon, sir, it doth, and yon grey lines
That fret the clouds are messengers of day.

Pardon me, sir, it is. The gray line over
there is the rising of the sun.

Casca

You shall confess that you are both deceived.
Here, as I point my sword, the Sun arises;
Which is a great way growing on the South,
Weighing the youthful season of the year.
Some two months hence, up higher toward the
North
He first presents his fire; and the high East
Stands, as the Capitol, directly here.

I think you are both wrong.
See where I'm pointing my sword. The sun is
rising in the south because of the time of year.
In two months, it will rise higher in the north.
The capitol is over there.

Brutus

Give me your hands all over, one by one.

Give me your hands, one over the other.

Cassius

And let us swear our resolution.

Let's swear an oath.

Brutus

No, not an oath: if not the face of men,
The sufferance of our souls, the time's abuse—
If these be motives weak, break off betimes,
And every man hence to his idle bed;
So let high-sighted tyranny range on,
Till each man drop by lottery. But if these,
As I am sure they do, bear fire enough
To kindle cowards, and to steel with valour
The melting spirits of women; then, countrymen,
What need we any spur but our own cause
To prick us to redress? what other bond
Than secret Romans, that have spoke the word,
And will not palter? and what other oath
Than honesty to honesty engaged,
That this shall be, or we will fall for it?
Swear priests, and cowards, and men cautelous,
Old feeble carrions, and such suffering souls
That welcome wrongs; unto bad causes swear
Such creatures as men doubt: but do not stain
The even virtue of our enterprise,
Nor th' insuppressive mettle of our spirits,
To think that or our cause or our performance
Did need an oath; when every drop of blood
That every Roman bears, and nobly bears,
Is guilty of a several bastardy,
If he do break the smallest particle
Of any promise that hath pass'd from him.

No, not an oath. We don't need to swear an oath to one another. Oaths are for cowards or old men. We have enough motivation to spur us to action. Our word is good enough.

Cassius

But what of Cicero? Shall we sound him?
I think he will stand very strong with us.

What about Cicero? Should we get him? I think he will support us.

Casca

Let us not leave him out.

Let's not leave him out.

Cinna

No, by no means.

No, by no means.

Metellus Cimber

O, let us have him! for his silver hairs
Will purchase us a good opinion,
And buy men's voices to commend our deeds:
It shall be said, his judgment ruled our hands;

Oh, let's include him. His age and wisdom will make us appear noteworthy and make men listen to us. He will also take the blame for our actions, since we are young.

Our youths and wildness shall no whit appear,
But all be buried in his gravity.

Brutus
O, name him not! let us not break with him;
For he will never follow any thing
That other men begin.

I don't think we should include him.
He'll never go along with anything like this.

Cassius
Then leave him out.

Then leave him out.

Casca
Indeed, he is not fit.

I don't think he is right.

Decius Brutus
Shall no man else be touch'd but only Caesar?

Are we only going after Caesar?

Cassius
Decius, well urged.--I think it is not meet,
Mark Antony, so well beloved of Caesar,
Should outlive Caesar: we shall find of him
A shrewd contriver; and you know his means,
If he improve them, may well stretch so far
As to annoy us all: which to prevent,
Let Antony and Caesar fall together.

Good question, Decius. I think Mark Antony
may give us some trouble. So, if he does,
let him fall with Caesar.

Brutus
Our course will seem too bloody, Caius Cassius,
To cut the head off, and then hack the limbs,
Like wrath in death, and envy afterwards;
For Antony is but a limb of Caesar.
Let us be sacrificers, but not butchers, Caius.
We all stand up against the spirit of Caesar;
And in the spirit of men there is no blood:
O, that we then could come by Caesar's spirit,
And not dismember Caesar! But, alas,
Caesar must bleed for it! And, gentle friends,
Let's kill him boldly, but not wrathfully;
Let's carve him as a dish fit for the gods,
Not hew him as a carcass fit for hounds;
And let our hearts, as subtle masters do,
Stir up their servants to an act of rage,
And after seem to chide 'em. This shall mark
Our purpose necessary, and not envious;
Which so appearing to the common eyes,
We shall be call'd purgers, not murderers.

I don't think that will be necessary, Cassius.
Antony just follows Caesar. With Caesar
gone, Antony will be no trouble. We must go
about this properly and not make Caesar seem
like a martyr. We do not want to be seen as
murderers, but purgers of evil.

And for Mark Antony, think not of him;
For he can do no more than Caesar's arm
When Caesar's head is off.

Cassius
Yet I do fear him;
For in th' ingrafted love he bears to Caesar--

I still fear him, because of his devotion to Caesar.

Brutus
Alas, good Cassius, do not think of him:
If he love Caesar, all that he can do
Is to himself,--take thought and die for Caesar.
And that were much he should; for he is given
To sports, to wildness, and much company.

Don't think of him, Cassius. If he loves Caesar, all he can do is die for him. He probably will die anyway the way he lives.

Trebonius
There is no fear in him; let him not die;
For he will live, and laugh at this hereafter.

No one should fear him. Don't kill him. He'll probably live and laugh about this later.

Clock strikes.

Brutus
Peace! count the clock.

Be quiet! What time is it?

Cassius
The clock hath stricken three.

Three o'clock.

Trebonius
'Tis time to part.

It's time to go.

Cassius
But it is doubtful yet
Whether Caesar will come forth today or no;
For he is superstitious grown of late,
Quite from the main opinion he held once
Of fantasy, of dreams, and ceremonies.
It may be these apparent prodigies,
The unaccustom'd terror of this night,
And the persuasion of his augurers
May hold him from the Capitol to-day.

We still don't know if Caesar will show in the Capitol today. He has been very superstitious lately.

Decius Brutus
Never fear that: if he be so resolved,
I can o'ersway him, for he loves to hear
That unicorns may be betray'd with trees,
And bears with glasses, elephants with holes,
Lions with toils, and men with flatterers:

Don't worry. I can get him to the Capitol. He loves to hear flattery, so I will get him there by flattering him.

But when I tell him he hates flatterers,
He says he does, being then most flattered.
Let me work; For I can give his humor the true bent,
And I will bring him to the Capitol.

Cassius
Nay, we will all of us be there to fetch him.

No, we will all go to get him.

Brutus
By the eighth hour: is that the uttermost?

By eight o'clock. Is that the time?

Cinna
Be that the uttermost; and fail not then.

I think so.

Metellus Cimber
Caius Ligarius doth bear Caesar hard,
Who rated him for speaking well of Pompey:
I wonder none of you have thought of him.

Caius Ligarius has reason to hate Caesar for
berating him when he spoke well of Pompey.
Have any of you thought about him?

Brutus
Now, good Metellus, go along by him:
He loves me well, and I have given him reason;
Send him but hither, and I'll fashion him.

Good, Metellus. Go get him. He loves me,
as well he should.
Send him here and I'll convince him.

Cassius
The morning comes upon 's.
We'll leave you, Brutus;--
And, friends, disperse yourselves, but all remember
What you have said, and show yourselves true
Romans.

The morning is here. We'll leave you, Brutus.
Friends, let's go our separate ways, but
remember what you have said here, and
show yourselves as true Romans.

Brutus
Good gentlemen, look fresh and merrily;
Let not our looks put on our purposes,
But bear it as our Roman actors do,
With untired spirits and formal constancy:
And so, good morrow to you every one.--

Good gentlemen, you must look fresh and
happy. You cannot let on our purpose with
your appearances. Let's be like Roman actors,
tireless spirits and well-composed faces.

Exit all but Brutus.

Boy! Lucius!--Fast asleep? It is no matter;
Enjoy the honey-heavy dew of slumber:
Thou hast no figures nor no fantasies,
Which busy care draws in the brains of men;
Therefore thou sleep'st so sound.

Boy! Lucius! Are you asleep? No matter.
Enjoy the heavenly state of sleep. You have
nothing to keep you from sleeping soundly.

Enter Portia

Portia
Brutus, my lord!

Brutus, my lord!

Brutus
Portia, what mean you? wherefore rise you now?
It is not for your health thus to commit
Your weak condition to the raw-cold morning.

Portia, what are you doing up? It's not healthy for you to be up in the cold morning air in your weak condition.

Portia
Nor for yours neither. You've ungently, Brutus,
Stole from my bed: and yesternight, at supper,
You suddenly arose, and walk'd about,
Musing and sighing, with your arms across;
And, when I ask'd you what the matter was,
You stared upon me with ungentle looks:
I urged you further; then you scratch'd your head,
And too impatiently stamp'd with your foot:
Yet I insisted, yet you answer'd not;
But, with an angry wafture of your hand,
Gave sign for me to leave you. So I did;
Fearing to strengthen that impatience
Which seem'd too much enkindled; and withal
Hoping it was but an effect of humour,
Which sometime hath his hour with every man.
It will not let you eat, nor talk, nor sleep;
And, could it work so much upon your shape
As it hath much prevail'd on your condition,
I should not know you, Brutus. Dear my lord,
Make me acquainted with your cause of grief.

It's not good for you, either. You urgently go up from bed, Brutus, and yesterday, at dinner, you suddenly got up and walked around thinking and sighing with your arms crossed. When I asked you what the matter was, you stared at me angrily. You stomped your foot when I inquired more. Then, you refused to answer me and waved me off. I don't know what is wrong with you, but you can't eat, or talk, or sleep. You're just not yourself, Brutus. Please, tell me what's wrong with you.

Brutus
I am not well in health, and that is all.

I just haven't been feeling well, lately.

Portia
Brutus is wise, and, were he not in health,
He would embrace the means to come by it.

You are a smart man, and if your health were compromised, you would seek treatment.

Brutus
Why, so I do. Good Portia, go to bed.

I am. Now, go to bed, dear Portia.

Portia
Is Brutus sick? and is it physical
To walk unbraced and suck up the humours

Are you sick? It can't be something physical, if you're walking around in the damp

Of the dank morning? What, is Brutus sick,
And will he steal out of his wholesome bed
To dare the vile contagion of the night,
And tempt the rheumy and unpurged air
To add unto his sickness? No, my Brutus;
You have some sick offense within your mind,
Which, by the right and virtue of my place,
I ought to know of: and, upon my knees,
I charge you, by my once commended beauty,
By all your vows of love, and that great vow
Which did incorporate and make us one,
That you unfold to me, yourself, your half,
Why you are heavy, and what men to-night
Have had resort to you; for here have been
Some six or seven, who did hide their faces
Even from darkness.

Brutus
Kneel not, gentle Portia.

Portia
I should not need, if you were gentle Brutus.
Within the bond of marriage, tell me, Brutus,
Is it excepted I should know no secrets
That appertain to you? Am I yourself
But, as it were, in sort or limitation,--
To keep with you at meals, comfort your bed,
And talk to you sometimes?
Dwell I but in the suburbs
Of your good pleasure? If it be no more,
Portia is Brutus' harlot, not his wife.

Brutus
You are my true and honorable wife;
As dear to me as are the ruddy drops
That visit my sad heart.

Portia
If this were true, then should I know this secret.
I grant I am a woman; but withal
A woman that Lord Brutus took to wife:
I grant I am a woman; but withal
A woman well reputed, Cato's daughter.
Think you I am no stronger than my sex,
Being so father'd and so husbanded?
Tell me your counsels, I will not disclose 'em.
I have made strong proof of my constancy,

*morning. And, what makes you get out of bed
to dare the germs that are in the night air.
No, Brutus, you are not sick, unless it is in
your mind. You are my husband, so I
know. Now, tell me why you are so
heavy-hearted. Who were the men you talking
to? I saw six or seven here in the dark.*

Don't ask, Portia.

*I wouldn't have to if you were honest to your
marriage vows. Tell me, Brutus. Am I not
to know everything about my husband?
Am I just supposed to spend time with you
at meals and at bedtime? If so, I'm not
your wife, I'm your whore.*

*You are my wonderful and honorable wife.
You are so dear to me.*

*If this is true, then I should know this secret.
Granted, I am just a woman, but I am the
woman you chose to be your wife.
I am the daughter of Cato, but you don't think
I am very strong. Tell me your secret and
I will not tell a soul. I have proven my
faithfulness, by giving myself a wound in
my thigh. If I can bear that pain, then I can
bear my husband's secrets.*

Giving myself a voluntary wound
Here in the thigh: can I bear that with patience
And not my husband's secrets?

Brutus
O ye gods, Render me worthy of this noble wife!

Oh, gods, make me worthy of this noble wife.

Knocking within.

Hark, hark, one knocks: Portia, go in awhile;
And by and by thy bosom shall partake
The secrets of my heart:
All my engagements I will construe to thee,
All the charactery of my sad brows.
Leave me with haste.

Hello! Someone is knocking, Portia. Please go in awhile, and I will come in and tell you what's going on. Hurry and leave.

Exit Portia.

--Lucius, who's that knocks?

Lucius, who's knocking?

Re-enter Lucius with Ligarius.

Lucius
Here is a sick man that would speak with you.

A sick man is here and he wants to speak with you.

Brutus
Caius Ligarius, that Metellus spake of.--
Boy, stand aside.--Caius Ligarius,--how?

Caius Ligarius, you are the one Metellus spoke of. Lucius, go away. How are you, Ligarius?

Ligarius
Vouchsafe good-morrow from a feeble tongue.

Good morning. I am not feeling well.

Brutus
O, what a time have you chose out, brave Caius,
To wear a kerchief! Would you were not sick!

What a time to be sick, brave Caius. You should cover your head and you would not be sick!

Ligarius
I am not sick, if Brutus have in hand
Any exploit worthy the name of honour.

I am not sick, if you have something worthy for me to do.

Brutus
Such an exploit have I in hand, Ligarius,
Had you a healthful ear to hear of it.

I do, if you are healthy enough to hear it.

Ligarius
By all the gods that Romans bow before,
I here discard my sickness. Soul of Rome!
Brave son, derived from honorable loins!
Thou, like an exorcist, hast conjured up
My mortified spirit. Now bid me run,
And I will strive with things impossible;
Yea, get the better of them. What's to do?

I swear by all the gods, I am no longer sick. You have made me well. Now, tell me what you want me to do.

Brutus

A piece of work that will make sick men whole.

What I am going to tell you may make sick men whole.

Ligarius
But are not some whole that we must make sick?

Will is making some healthy men sick?

Brutus
That must we also. What it is, my Caius,
I shall unfold to thee, as we are going,
To whom it must be done.

It may, also. I will tell you as we go to whom it must be done.

Ligarius
Set on your foot;
And with a heart new-fired I follow you,
To do I know not what: but it sufficeth
That Brutus leads me on.

I'm following you, although I still don't know why. But as long as you're leading, I'm following.

Brutus
Follow me then.

Come this way, then.

Exit.

Scene II: Caesar's house.

Thunder and lightning. Enter Caesar, in his night-gown.

Caesar
Nor heaven nor earth have been at peace tonight:
Thrice hath Calpurnia in her sleep cried out,
"Help, ho! They murder Caesar!"--Who's within?

Neither heaven nor earth is at peace this night. Three times Calpurnia has cried out in her sleep, "Help! They murder Caesar!" Who's there?

Servant
My lord?

Your servant, my lord?

Caesar
Go bid the priests do present sacrifice,
And bring me their opinions of success.

Tell the priests to present a sacrifice and come tell me what they think.

Servant
I will, my lord.

I will, my lord.

Exit.

Enter Calpurnia.

Calpurnia
What mean you, Caesar? Think you to walk forth?
You shall not stir out of your house to-day.

What's going on, Caesar? Do you mean to go out today? You shouldn't.

Caesar
Caesar shall forth: the things that threaten me
Ne'er look but on my back; when they shall see
The face of Caesar, they are vanished.

I am going out because those that wish to cause me harm always talk behind my back. When I appear, they vanish.

Calpurnia
Caesar, I never stood on ceremonies,
Yet now they fright me. There is one within,
Besides the things that we have heard and seen,
Recounts most horrid sights seen by the watch.
A lioness hath whelped in the streets;
And graves have yawn'd, and yielded up their dead;
Fierce fiery warriors fight upon the clouds,
In ranks and squadrons and right form of war,
Which drizzled blood upon the Capitol;

Caesar, I have never been superstitious, but now I am frightened. A lioness was seen in the streets, graves have opened revealing the dead, fire has been set throughout the Capitol, and the noise of battle heard in the air with the cries of horses, dying men, and shrieking ghosts. Oh, Caesar! There is no explanation for these occurrences, and I am afraid.

The noise of battle hurtled in the air,
Horses did neigh, and dying men did groan;
And ghosts did shriek and squeal about the streets.
O Caesar,these things are beyond all use,
And I do fear them!

Caesar
What can be avoided
Whose end is purposed by the mighty gods?
Yet Caesar shall go forth; for these predictions
Are to the world in general as to Caesar.

Who can avoid what the gods ordain? So, I shall go out and face these predictions for myself and for Rome.

Calpurnia
When beggars die, there are no comets seen;
The heavens themselves blaze forth the death
of princes.

When beggars die, nothing extraordinary happens, but when a prince dies, strange things are seen.

Caesar
Cowards die many times before their deaths;
The valiant never taste of death but once.
Of all the wonders that I yet have heard,
It seems to me most strange that men should fear;
Seeing that death, a necessary end,
Will come when it will come.--

Cowards die many deaths, but a courageous man only experiences death once. Death is inevitable, so I don't understand why men fear it.

Re-enter Servant.

What say the augurers?

What did the priests say?

Servant
They would not have you to stir forth to-day.
Plucking the entrails of an offering forth,
They could not find a heart within the beast.

They don't think you should come out today. When they performed the sacrifice, they couldn't find the heart.

Caesar
The gods do this in shame of cowardice:
Caesar should be a beast without a heart,
If he should stay at home today for fear.
No, Caesar shall not: danger knows full well
That Caesar is more dangerous than he:
We are two lions litter'd in one day,
And I the elder and more terrible;
And Caesar shall go forth.

It is a sign from the gods, that a beast without a heart is a coward. I will not stay home today in fear. I, myself, am dangerous. So, I will go.

Calpurnia
Alas, my lord,
Your wisdom is consumed in confidence!

Please, my lord, don't go. Blame it on my fear. Let Mark Antony go instead, and say

Do not go forth to-day: call it my fear
That keeps you in the house, and not your own.
We'll send Mark Antony to the Senate-house,
And he shall say you are not well to-day:
Let me, upon my knee, prevail in this.

that you are ill. I am begging you. Do not go.

Caesar
Mark Antony shall say I am not well,
And, for thy humor, I will stay at home.

Mark Antony can say I am not well,
and I will stay home for you.

Enter Decius Brutus

Here's Decius Brutus, he shall tell them so.

Here's Decius Brutus. He can tell them.

Decius Brutus
Caesar, all hail! Good morrow, worthy Caesar:
I come to fetch you to the Senate-house.

All hail, Caesar! Good morning, sir.
I have come to escort you to the senate-house.

Caesar
And you are come in very happy time
To bear my greeting to the Senators,
And tell them that I will not come to-day.
Cannot, is false; and that I dare not, falser:
I will not come to-day. Tell them so, Decius.

I am glad you are here. You can tell the
senators that I will not be coming today, well
cannot is not really true, nor is I dare not.
Just tell them I'm not coming.

Calpurnia
Say he is sick.

Say he is sick.

Caesar
Shall Caesar send a lie?
Have I in conquest stretch'd mine arm so far,
To be afeard to tell grey-beards the truth?—
Decius, go tell them Caesar will not come.

Shall I tell a lie? Am I afraid to tell the old
men the truth? Decius, go tell I am not
coming.

Decius Brutus
Most mighty Caesar, let me know some cause,
Lest I be laugh'd at when I tell them so.

You must give me a reason, so I will not be
laughed at.

Caesar
The cause is in my will; I will not come:
That is enough to satisfy the Senate.
But, for your private satisfaction,
Because I love you, I will let you know:
Calpurnia here, my wife, stays me at home:
She dreamt to-night she saw my statua,
Which, like a fountain with an hundred spouts,

Just tell them I don't want to come.
That should be enough. But, since I love you,
I will tell you in private,
Calpurnia had a dream and saw me
murdered. She has begged me to stay home
today.

Did run pure blood; and many lusty Romans
Came smiling and did bathe their hands in it:
And these does she apply for warnings and portents
And evils imminent; and on her knee
Hath begg'd that I will stay at home to-day.

Decius Brutus

This dream is all amiss interpreted:
It was a vision fair and fortunate.
Your statue spouting blood in many pipes,
In which so many smiling Romans bathed,
Signifies that from you great Rome shall suck
Reviving blood; and that great men shall press
For tinctures, stains, relics, and cognizance.
This by Calpurnia's dream is signified.

The dream is misinterpreted. It was not the blood of your death but the blood of birth. Rome is going to experience a revival under you. This is what Calpurnia's dream meant.

Caesar

And this way have you well expounded it.

That is a good explanation.

Decius Brutus

I have, when you have heard what I can say;
And know it now: The Senate have concluded
To give this day a crown to mighty Caesar.
If you shall send them word you will not come,
Their minds may change. Besides, it were a mock
Apt to be render'd, for someone to say
"Break up the Senate till another time,
When Caesar's wife shall meet with better dreams."
If Caesar hide himself, shall they not whisper
"Lo, Caesar is afraid"?
Pardon me, Caesar; for my dear dear love
To your proceeding bids me tell you this;
And reason to my love is liable.

I know because today the senate decided to give you a crown. If you don't come, they may change their minds. Some may even question your abilities if you listen to your wife's dreams. Pardon my frankness, I tell you this out of my love for you.

Caesar

How foolish do your fears seem now, Calpurnia!
I am ashamed I did yield to them.
Give me my robe, for I will go.

See, Calpurnia, how foolish fear is. I ashamed I listened to them. Give me my robe, and I will go.

Enter Publius, Brutus, Ligarius, Metellus, Casca, Trebonius, and Cinna.

And look where Publius is come to fetch me.

Now, Publius has come to get me.

Publius

Good morrow, Caesar.

Good morning, Caesar.

Caesar
Welcome, Publius.—
What, Brutus, are you stirr'd so early too?—
Good morrow, Casca.--Caius Ligarius,
Caesar was ne'er so much your enemy
As that same ague which hath made you lean.—
What is't o'clock?

Welcome, Publius. What are you doing up so early, Brutus? Good morning, Casca. Caius Ligarius, you are looking sickly. What time is it?

Brutus
Caesar, 'tis strucken eight.

Caesar, it's eight o'clock.

Caesar
I thank you for your pains and courtesy.

Thank you.

Enter Antony.

See! Antony, that revels long o'nights,
Is notwithstanding up.--Good morrow, Antony.

Even the partier, Antony, is up. Good morning, Antony!

Antony
So to most noble Caesar.

Same to you, most noble Caesar.

Caesar
Bid them prepare within:
I am to blame to be thus waited for.—
Now, Cinna;--now, Metellus;--what, Trebonius!
I have an hour's talk in store for you:
Remember that you call on me to-day;
Be near me, that I may remember you.

Tell them to get ready and that I am to blame for keeping them waiting. Cinna, Mettellus, and Trebonius, I have a long talk prepared for you, so stay close by.

Trebonius
Caesar, I will. [Aside.] and so near will I be,
That your best friends shall wish I had been
further.

I will, Caesar.
Aside.
I will be so close that your best friends will wish I had been further away.

Caesar
Good friends, go in, and taste some wine with me;
And we, like friends, will straightway go together.

My good friends, let's go in and drink some wine and then, we will go together.

Brutus
[Aside.]
That every like is not the same, O Caesar,
The heart of Brutus yearns to think upon!

Aside.
I wish things could be the same, Caesar. I hate to think of the future.

Exit all.

Scene III: A street near the Capitol.

Enter Artemidorus, reading a paper.

Artemidorus
"Caesar, beware of Brutus; take heed of Cassius;
come not near Casca; have an eye to Cinna; trust
not Trebonius; mark well Metellus Cimber;
Decius Brutus loves thee not; thou hast wrong'd
Caius Ligarius. There is but one mind in all
these men, and it is bent against Caesar. If thou
be'st not immortal, look about you: security
gives way to conspiracy. The mighty gods
defend thee! Thy lover, Artemidorus."
Here will I stand till Caesar pass along,
And as a suitor will I give him this.
My heart laments that virtue cannot live
Out of the teeth of emulation.—
If thou read this, O Caesar, thou mayest live;
If not, the Fates with traitors do contrive.

Exit.

"Caesar, beware of Brutus and take heed of Cassius. Do not go near Casca, and keep an eye on Cinna. Don't trust Trebonius or Metellus Cimber. Decius Brutus doesn't love you, and you have the wrong idea about Caius Ligarius. These men are of one mind and it is anti-Caesar. If you are not immortal, look around and recognize the conspiracy. May the mighty gods defend you. Your friend, Artemidorus." I will stand here until Caesar passes by and give him this. My heart aches that a good man cannot be without enemies. If Caesar reads this, he may live. If not, then Fate conspires with traitors.

Scene IV: Another part of the same street, before the house of Brutus.

Enter Portia and Lucius.

Portia
I pr'ythee, boy, run to the Senate-house;
Stay not to answer me, but get thee gone.
Why dost thou stay?

*Please, boy, run to the senate-house
Get going. Why are you still here?*

Lucius
To know my errand, madam.

I need to know why I'm going, madam.

Portia
I would have had thee there, and here again,
Ere I can tell thee what thou shouldst do there.—
[Aside.] O constancy, be strong upon my side!
Set a huge mountain 'tween my heart and tongue!
I have a man's mind, but a woman's might.
How hard it is for women to keep counsel!—
Art thou here yet?

*You could have been there and back again
by the time I can tell you what you are to do
there. Oh Lord, help me be strong. Keep my
heart from controlling my mouth. It is so hard
for a woman to keep a secret. Are you still
here?*

Lucius
Madam, what should I do?
Run to the Capitol, and nothing else?
And so return to you, and nothing else?

*Madam, what do you want me to do?
Just go there and back, nothing else?*

Portia
Yes, bring me word, boy, if thy lord look well,
For he went sickly forth: and take good note
What Caesar doth, what suitors press to him.
Hark, boy! what noise is that?

*Yes, bring me word, boy, if your lord looked
okay. He was sick when he went. Also, take
a look at Caesar, and see what men are near
him. Listen, boy! What was that noise?*

Lucius
I hear none, madam.

I didn't hear anything.

Portia
Pr'ythee, listen well:
I heard a bustling rumour, like a fray,
And the wind brings it from the Capitol.

*Please listen harder.
I heard a bustling noise from the direction of
the Capitol.*

Enter the Soothsayer.

Portia

Come hither, fellow: Which way hast thou been?

Come here, fellow. Where are you coming from?

Soothsayer
At mine own house, good lady.

From my house, good lady.

Portia
What is't o'clock?

What time is it?

Soothsayer
About the ninth hour, lady.

It's about nine o'clock.

Portia
Is Caesar yet gone to the Capitol?

Has Caesar gone to the Capitol, yet?

Soothsayer
Madam, not yet: I go to take my stand
To see him pass on to the Capitol.

Not yet, madam. I haven't seen him pass by.

Portia
Thou hast some suit to Caesar, hast thou not?

You work for Caesar, right?

Soothsayer
That I have, lady: if it will please Caesar
To be so good to Caesar as to hear me,
I shall beseech him to befriend himself.

Yes. When it pleases him to hear me out, I am a friend to him.

Portia
Why, know'st thou any harm's intended towards him?

Do you know of any harm intended towards him?

Soothsayer
None that I know will be, much that I fear may chance.
Good morrow to you.--Here the street is narrow:
The throng that follows Caesar at the heels,
Of Senators, of Praetors, common suitors,
Will crowd a feeble man almost to death:
I'll get me to a place more void, and there
Speak to great Caesar as he comes along.

None that I know of, although I fear there may be a chance. Good day to you. I need to get going before Caesar and his followers come through this narrow street and trample me to death. I need to get to a better place so I may speak to Caesar.

Exit.

Portia
I must go in.--[Aside.] Ah me, how weak a thing
The heart of woman is!--O Brutus,
The heavens speed thee in thine enterprise!—

I must go inside. Yes, the heart of a woman is is weak. Oh Brutus, may the heavens help you in your work. I know the boy heard me. Brutus

Sure, the boy heard me.--Brutus hath a suit
That Caesar will not grant.--O, I grow faint.—
Run, Lucius, and commend me to my lord;
Say I am merry: come to me again,
And bring me word what he doth say to thee.

has a request Caesar will not grant.
Oh, I grow weaker.
Run, Lucius, and tell my lord I am well and
happy. Then, come to me and tell me what he
says

Act III

Scene I: Rome. Before the Capitol with the Senate sitting above.

A crowd of people: Artemidorus and the Soothsayer. Flourish. Enter Caesar, Brutus, Cassius, Casca, Decius Brutus, Metellus Cimber, Trebonius, Cinna, Mark Antony, Lepidus, Popilius, Publius, and others.

Caesar
To the Soothsayer.
The Ides of March are come.

The ides of March have come.

Soothsayer
Ay, Caesar; but not gone.

Yes, but they are not gone.

Artemidorus
Hail, Caesar! read this schedule.

Hail, Caesar! Read this schedule.

Decius Brutus
Trebonius doth desire you to o'er-read,
At your best leisure, this his humble suit.

Trebonius needs you to read over this petition, when you get a moment.

Artemidorus
O Caesar, read mine first; for mine's a suit
That touches Caesar nearer: read it, great Caesar.

Oh Caesar, read mine first. My petition is more personal. Read it, great Caesar.

Caesar
What touches us ourself shall be last served.

If it has something to do with me, I'll read it last.

Artemidorus
Delay not, Caesar; read it instantly.

Don't delay, Caesar. Read it, now.

Caesar
What, is the fellow mad?

Have you gone crazy?

Publius
Sirrah, give place.

Stand back, sir.

Cassius
What, urge you your petitions in the street?
Come to the Capitol.

Caesar goes up to the Senate-House and the rest follows.

Popilius
I wish your enterprise to-day may thrive.

Cassius
What enterprise, Popilius?

Popilius
Fare you well. Advances to Caesar.

Advances towards Caesar.

Brutus
What said Popilius Lena?

Cassius
He wish'd to-day our enterprise might thrive.
I fear our purpose is discovered.

Brutus
Look, how he makes to Caesar: mark him.

Cassius
Casca, be sudden, for we fear prevention.—
Brutus, what shall be done? If this be known,
Cassius or Caesar never shall turn back,
For I will slay myself.

Brutus
Cassius, be constant:
Popilius Lena speaks not of our purposes;
For, look, he smiles, and Caesar doth not change.

Cassius
Trebonius knows his time, for, look you, Brutus,
He draws Mark Antony out of the way.

Exit Antony and Trebonius.

Decius Brutus
Where is Metellus Cimber? Let him go,

Are you petitioning in the streets?
Come to the Capitol.

I hope your work goes well today.

What work, Popilius?

Goodbye then.

What did Popilius Lena say?

He hoped our work would go well today
I'm afraid he knows what we're planning.

Look how he is getting closer to Caesar.
Watch him.

Casca, act quickly. We don't want to be
prevented. Brutus, what should we do?
If we are discovered, I will kill myself.

Be calm, Cassius. Popilius Lena is not talking
about our plan. Look at him smiling, and
Caesar's expression has not changed.

Trebonius knows what to do.
He is drawing Mark Antony away.

Where is Metellus Cimber? Let him go

And presently prefer his suit to Caesar.

Brutus

He is address'd; press near and second him.

and present his case to Caesar.

He is presenting. Go closer and help him.

Cinna

Casca, you are the first that rears your hand.

Casca, you are the first to strike.

Caesar

What is now amiss
That Caesar and his Senate must redress?

Are we all ready?
What do the senate and I need to address?

Metellus Cimber

Most high, most mighty, and most puissant Caesar,
Metellus Cimber throws before thy seat
An humble heart.

Most high and mighty Caesar, I throw myself
at your feet with a humble heart…

Kneeling.

Caesar

I must prevent thee, Cimber.
These couchings and these lowly courtesies
Might fire the blood of ordinary men,
And turn pre-ordinance and first decree
Into the law of children. Be not fond,
To think that Caesar bears such rebel blood
That will be thaw'd from the true quality
With that which melteth fools; I mean, sweet words,
Low-crooked curtsies, and base spaniel-fawning.
Thy brother by decree is banished:
If thou dost bend, and pray, and fawn for him,
I spurn thee like a cur out of my way.
Know, Caesar doth not wrong, nor without cause
Will he be satisfied.

No need, Cimber. Your actions may make men
think that I'm persuaded by such flattery.
Your brother has been banished, and I will
not grant him a pardon without a good
reason. Caesar did never wrong but with
just cause, Nor without cause will he be
satisfied.

Metellus Cimber

Is there no voice more worthy than my own,
To sound more sweetly in great Caesar's ear
For the repealing of my banish'd brother?

Isn't my voice enough to petition for
my brother's pardon?

Brutus

I kiss thy hand, but not in flattery, Caesar;
Desiring thee that Publius Cimber may
Have an immediate freedom of repeal.

I kiss your hand, not out of flattery, but to
show my desire that you grant Publius
Cimber's claim to freedom.

Caesar

What, Brutus?

What, Brutus!

Cassius
Pardon, Caesar; Caesar, pardon:
As low as to thy foot doth Cassius fall,
To beg enfranchisement for Publius Cimber.

Pardon me, Caesar. I bow at your feet to plea for Publius Cimber.

Caesar
I could be well moved, if I were as you;
If I could pray to move, prayers would move me:
But I am constant as the northern star,
Of whose true-fix'd and resting quality
There is no fellow in the firmament.
The skies are painted with unnumber'd sparks,
They are all fire, and every one doth shine;
But there's but one in all doth hold his place:
So in the world; 'tis furnish'd well with men,
And men are flesh and blood, and apprehensive;
Yet in the number I do know but one
That unassailable holds on his rank,
Unshaked of motion: and that I am he,
Let me a little show it, even in this,--
That I was constant Cimber should be banish'd,
And constant do remain to keep him so.

I could be convinced if, I were you. But I am as immovable as the North Star. They are all made of fire, but only one remains unmoving. It is the same with men. I am the only one who will not be moved. I remain firm in my decision.

Cinna
O Caesar,--

Oh, Caesar...

Caesar
Hence! wilt thou lift up Olympus?

What do you want me to do? Lift up Mount Olympus?

Decius Brutus
Great Caesar,--

Great Caesar...

Caesar
Doth not Brutus bootless kneel?

Didn't Brutus beg for him?

Casca
Speak, hands, for me!

Hands, speak for me!

Casca first, then the other Conspirators and Brutus stab Caesar.

Caesar
Et tu, Brute?-- Then fall, Caesar!

And you, Brute! Then, die Caesar!

Dies.

Cinna

Liberty! Freedom! Tyranny is dead!—
Run hence, proclaim, cry it about the streets.

Cassius
Some to the common pulpits and cry out,
"Liberty, freedom, and enfranchisement!"

Brutus
People and Senators, be not affrighted;
Fly not; stand still; ambition's debt is paid.

Casca
Go to the pulpit, Brutus.

Decius Brutus
And Cassius too.

Brutus
Where's Publius?

Cinna
Here, quite confounded with this mutiny.

Metellus Cimber
Stand fast together, lest some friend of Caesar's
Should chance--

Brutus
Talk not of standing.--Publius, good cheer!
There is no harm intended to your person,
Nor to no Roman else: so tell them, Publius.

Cassius
And leave us, Publius; lest that the people
Rushing on us, should do your age some mischief.

Brutus
Do so;--and let no man abide this deed
But we the doers.

Re-enter Trebonius.

Cassius
Where's Antony?

Trebonius

---

*Liberty! Freedom! Tyranny is dead!
Run and proclaim it in the streets.*

*Go to the commons and cry out,
"Liberty, freedom, and democracy!"*

*Don't be afraid, people and senators. Don't
run off. Stay because Caesar was killed by his
ambition.*

Go to the pulpit, Brutus.

And Cassius, too.

Where's Publius?

He's here and quite confused with the mutiny.

*Stand by each other, or else some friend of
Caesar's may...*

*Don't talk like that. Publius, be happy.
No harm is meant for you or any other
Roman. Tell them Publius.*

*Leave us, Publius, in case the people coming
towards us should harm you.*

*Go ahead. No one will claim this deed except
those who did it.*

Where is Antony?

Fled to his house amazed.
Men, wives, and children stare, cry out, and run,
As it were doomsday.

Brutus
Fates, we will know your pleasures:
That we shall die, we know; 'tis but the time
And drawing days out, that men stand upon.

Cassius
Why, he that cuts off twenty years of life
Cuts off so many years of fearing death.

Brutus
Grant that, and then is death a benefit:
So are we Caesar's friends, that have abridged
His time of fearing death.--Stoop, Romans, stoop,
And let us bathe our hands in Caesar's blood
Up to the elbows, and besmear our swords:
Then walk we forth, even to the market-place,
And waving our red weapons o'er our heads,
Let's all cry, "Peace, freedom, and liberty!"

Cassius
Stoop then, and wash. How many ages hence
Shall this our lofty scene be acted o'er
In States unborn and accents yet unknown!

Brutus
How many times shall Caesar bleed in sport,
That now on Pompey's basis lies along
No worthier than the dust!

Cassius
So oft as that shall be,
So often shall the knot of us be call'd
The men that gave their country liberty

Decius Brutus
What, shall we forth?

Cassius
Ay, every man away:
Brutus shall lead; and we will grace his heels
With the most boldest and best hearts of Rome.

He ran to his house, awestruck. Men, wives, and children cry out and run like it is the end of the world.

We will soon know what Fate has in store for us. We will all die someday, although, we will try to postpone it.

If one cuts off twenty years from his life, that's twenty years he doesn't fear death.

That's true, so we are Caesar's friends because we have shortened his life of fearing death. Bend, gentlemen, and soak your hands in Caesar's blood up to the elbow. Smear the blood on your sword, and let's walk to the market-place and cry, "Peace, freedom, and liberty."

Bend and wash yourselves in Caesar's blood How many times will our scene be repeated around the world!

How many times will this be replayed even though Caesar now lies in the dirt!

However many times, we will be the men who freed their fellow countrymen.

Shall we go?

*Yes, let's go everyone.
Brutus leads and we will follow him, the boldest men in all of Rome.*

Enter a servant.

Brutus
Soft, who comes here?

Shh! Who is this? A friend of Antony's.

Servant
Thus, Brutus, did my master bid me kneel;
Thus did Mark Antony bid me fall down;
And, being prostrate, thus he bade me say:
Brutus is noble, wise, valiant, and honest;
Caesar was mighty, bold, royal, and loving;
Say I love Brutus and I honor him;
Say I fear'd Caesar, honour'd him, and loved him.
If Brutus will vouchsafe that Antony
May safely come to him, and be resolved
How Caesar hath deserved to lie in death,
Mark Antony shall not love Caesar dead
So well as Brutus living; but will follow
The fortunes and affairs of noble Brutus
Thorough the hazards of this untrod state
With all true faith. So says my master Antony.

Brutus, my master told me to kneel.
Mark Antony told me to fall down and say,
"Brutus is noble wise, valiant, and honest.
Caesar was mighty, bold, royal, and loving.
love Brutus and I honor him. I was afraid of
Caesar, but I honored and loved him.
If Brutus can promise his safety, Antony will
come to him and listen to how Caesar came to
deserve to die. Mark Antony will not love
Caesar, dead, more than the living Brutus.
He will follow Brutus and be faithful to him."

Brutus
Thy master is a wise and valiant Roman;
I never thought him worse.
Tell him, so please him come unto this place,
He shall be satisfied and, by my honour,
Depart untouch'd.

Your master is a wise and brave Roman.
I never thought poorly of him. Tell him to
come here and he will not be touched.

Servant
I'll fetch him presently.

I will go get him right now.

Exit.

Brutus
I know that we shall have him well to friend.

It will benefit us to have him as a friend.

Cassius
I wish we may: but yet have I a mind
That fears him much; and my misgiving still
Falls shrewdly to the purpose.

I hope so, but I am afraid of him.

Brutus
But here comes Antony.--

Here he comes.

Re-enter Antony.

Welcome, Mark Antony.

Welcome, Mark Antony.

Antony
O mighty Caesar! Dost thou lie so low?
Are all thy conquests, glories, triumphs, spoils,
Shrunk to this little measure? Fare thee well.—
I know not, gentlemen, what you intend,
Who else must be let blood, who else is rank:
If I myself, there is no hour so fit
As Caesar's death-hour, nor no instrument
Of half that worth as those your swords, made rich
With the most noble blood of all this world.
I do beseech ye, if you bear me hard,
Now, whilst your purpled hands do reek and smoke,
Fulfill your pleasure. Live a thousand years,
I shall not find myself so apt to die:
No place will please me so, no means of death,
As here by Caesar, and by you cut off,
The choice and master spirits of this age.

Oh mighty Caesar! You lie so low.
All of your triumphs and glories have some
to this. Goodbye. I do not know what you
gentlemen are thinking, but who else has to
die? Me? If so, now's the time. Do it with
those swords drenched in noble blood. I beg
you, if you have something against me, take
care of it now. If I live a thousand years,
I will not be more prepared to die as I am
right now. No place will please me more,
as to die by Caesar.

Brutus
O Antony, beg not your death of us!
Though now we must appear bloody and cruel,
As, by our hands and this our present act
You see we do; yet see you but our hands
And this the bleeding business they have done:
Our hearts you see not; they are pitiful;
And pity to the general wrong of Rome--
As fire drives out fire, so pity pity--
Hath done this deed on Caesar. For your part,
To you our swords have leaden points,
Mark Antony;
Our arms in strength of amity, and our hearts
Of brothers' temper, do receive you in
With all kind love, good thoughts, and reverence.

Oh, Antony, don't beg us to kill you.
I know we must appear bloody and cruel,
but you do not know our hearts. They are sad
and sad for Rome. You see our swords, Mark
Antony, and you see malice, but we receive
you with love and acceptance.

Cassius
Your voice shall be as strong as any man's
In the disposing of new dignities.

You will be as strong as any man
in the development of a new senate.

Brutus
Only be patient till we have appeased

Only be patient while we take care of the

The multitude, beside themselves with fear,
And then we will deliver you the cause
Why I, that did love Caesar when I struck him,
Have thus proceeded.

Antony
I doubt not of your wisdom.
Let each man render me his bloody hand:
First, Marcus Brutus, will I shake with you;--
Next, Caius Cassius, do I take your hand;--
Now, Decius Brutus, yours;--now yours, Metellus;--
Yours, Cinna;--and, my valiant Casca, yours;--
Though last, not least in love, yours, good
Trebonius.
Gentlemen all--alas, what shall I say?
My credit now stands on such slippery ground,
That one of two bad ways you must conceit me,
Either a coward or a flatterer.—
That I did love thee, Caesar, O, 'tis true:
If then thy spirit look upon us now,
Shall it not grieve thee dearer than thy death
To see thy Antony making his peace,
Shaking the bloody fingers of thy foes,--
Most noble!--in the presence of thy corse?
Had I as many eyes as thou hast wounds,
Weeping as fast as they stream forth thy blood,
It would become me better than to close
In terms of friendship with thine enemies.
Pardon me, Julius! Here wast thou bay'd, brave hart;
Here didst thou fall; and here thy hunters stand,
Sign'd in thy spoil, and crimson'd in thy death.--
O world, thou wast the forest to this hart;
And this, indeed, O world, the heart of thee.--
How like a deer strucken by many princes,
Dost thou here lie!

Cassius
Mark Antony,--

Antony
Pardon me, Caius Cassius:
The enemies of Caesar shall say this;
Then, in a friend, it is cold modesty.

Cassius
I blame you not for praising Caesar so;

people who are beside themselves with fear.
Then, we will tell you why we killed Caesar.

I don't doubt your wisdom. Let me shake each of your hands, first, Marcus Brutus and Caius Cassius. Now, Decius Brutus give me your hand and Metellus. Let me shake yours, Cinna and brave Casca. Last but not least, give me your hand Trebonius. What can I say, gentlemen? You must be unsure of how to take me, coward or flatterer. I did love Caesar, and if his spirit is watching us now, I hope he is not grieved by me making peace with his enemies. If I had as many eyes as you have wounds, I would still look better than the act of becoming friends with your murderers. Forgive me, Julius! Here, you were hunted and killed like a deer, stabbed by the swords of many princes!

Mark Antony...

Forgive me, Caius Cassius.
Even the enemies of Caesar would say the same thing.

I don't blame you for praising Caesar,

But what compact mean you to have with us?
Will you be prick'd in number of our friends,
Or shall we on, and not depend on you?

but what is your purpose? Are you our friend or can't we depend on you.

Antony
Therefore I took your hands; but was indeed
Sway'd from the point, by looking down on Caesar.
Friends am I with you all, and love you all,
Upon this hope, that you shall give me reasons
Why and wherein Caesar was dangerous.

I took your hands in friendship, but lost my focus when I saw Caesar. I am with you all, and I love you. I hope you can entrust in me your reasons for killing Caesar.

Brutus
Or else were this a savage spectacle:
Our reasons are so full of good regard
That were you, Antony, the son of Caesar,
You should be satisfied.

We had such noble intentions, that even if you were Caesar's son you'd be pleased.

Antony
That's all I seek:
And am moreover suitor that I may
Produce his body to the market-place;
And in the pulpit, as becomes a friend,
Speak in the order of his funeral.

That's all I want to know, and I'd like to take his body to the pulpit, like a friend would, and speak at his funeral.

Brutus
You shall, Mark Antony.

You will, Mark Antony.

Cassius
Brutus, a word with you.

Brutus, can I have a word with you.

Aside to Brutus.

You know not what you do; do not consent
That Antony speak in his funeral:
Know you how much the people may be moved
By that which he will utter?

You don't know what you are doing. Don't allow Antony to speak at his funeral. You don't know how the people will be affected by what he will say.

Brutus
By your pardon: I will myself into the pulpit first,
And show the reason of our Caesar's death:
What Antony shall speak, I will protest
He speaks by leave and by permission;
And that we are contented Caesar shall
Have all true rights and lawful ceremonies.
It shall advantage more than do us wrong.

I beg your pardon, but I will speak first and tell everyone why we killed Caesar. I will counter anything Antony will say, but we must allow Caesar to have all the ceremony and rites of someone in his position. It will be to our advantage.

Cassius

I know not what may fall; I like it not.

I don't know what will happen, and I don't like it at all.

Brutus

Mark Antony, here, take you Caesar's body.
You shall not in your funeral speech blame us,
But speak all good you can devise of Caesar;
And say you do't by our permission;
Else shall you not have any hand at all
About his funeral: and you shall speak
In the same pulpit whereto I am going,
After my speech is ended.

Mark Antony, take Caesar's body.
You may not blame us in your funeral speech.
Speak well of Caesar, and let everyone know
we've given you permission to speak or else
you won't be able to speak at all.
You are going to speak after me.

Antony

Be it so; I do desire no more.

That's fine. That's all I want.

Brutus

Prepare the body, then, and follow us.

Prepare the body then, and follow us.

Exit all but Antony.

Antony

O, pardon me, thou bleeding piece of earth,
That I am meek and gentle with these butchers!
Thou art the ruins of the noblest man
That ever lived in the tide of times.
Woe to the hand that shed this costly blood!
Over thy wounds now do I prophesy,--
Which, like dumb mouths do ope their ruby lips
To beg the voice and utterance of my tongue,--
A curse shall light upon the limbs of men;
Domestic fury and fierce civil strife
Shall cumber all the parts of Italy;
Blood and destruction shall be so in use,
And dreadful objects so familiar,
That mothers shall but smile when they behold
Their infants quarter'd with the hands of war;
All pity choked with custom of fell deeds:
And Caesar's spirit, ranging for revenge,
With Ate' by his side come hot from Hell,
Shall in these confines with a monarch's voice
Cry "Havoc!" and let slip the dogs of war,
That this foul deed shall smell above the earth
With carrion men, groaning for burial.—

Forgive me, Caesar that I am meek and gentle
with these butchers! You were the noblest man
who ever lived. I curse the hand that shed
your blood! Over your wounds I swear a curse
upon their lives. Domestic fury and fierce civil
strife will erupt all over Italy. It will be so
awful and become so customary that mothers
will smile when their infants are torn apart.
Caesar's spirit will get revenge as it cries in
a kingly voice, "Havoc," and the dogs of war
are released. Dying men will groan to be
buried.

Enter a servant.

You serve Octavius Caesar, do you not?

You are a servant for Octavius Caesar, aren't you?

Servant
I do, Mark Antony.

I am, Mark Antony.

Antony
Caesar did write for him to come to Rome.

Caesar wrote to him and asked him to come to Rome.

Servant
He did receive his letters, and is coming;
And bid me say to you by word of mouth,--
[Seeing the body.] O Caesar!--

He did receive his letters and is coming.
He asked me to tell you... Oh, Caesar!
Sees the body.

Antony
Thy heart is big, get thee apart and weep.
Passion, I see, is catching; for mine eyes,
Seeing those beads of sorrow stand in thine,
Began to water. Is thy master coming?

Your heart is big. Go ahead and cry.
The passion I see in your eyes is contagious
for now my eyes are watering.
Is your master coming?

Servant
He lies tonight within seven leagues of Rome.

He is with seven Roman battalions tonight.

Antony
Post back with speed, and tell him what hath
chanced.
Here is a mourning Rome, a dangerous Rome,
No Rome of safety for Octavius yet;
Hie hence, and tell him so. Yet stay awhile;
Thou shalt not back till I have borne this corse
Into the market-place: there shall I try,
In my oration, how the people take
The cruel issue of these bloody men;
According to the which thou shalt discourse
To young Octavius of the state of things.
Lend me your hand.

Go back quickly and tell him what has
happened.
Rome is dangerous and not safe for Octavius,
yet. No, stay awhile. Don't leave until I take
the body to the market-place. We will see how
the people respond to this bloody event. Then
you can let Octavius know how things are.
Give me a hand.

Exit with Caesar's body.

Scene II: The forum.

Enter Brutus, Cassius, and a throng of Citizens

Citizens
We will be satisfied; let us be satisfied.

Tell us something to satisfy us.

Brutus
Then follow me, and give me audience, friends.—
Cassius, go you into the other street
And part the numbers.--
Those that will hear me speak, let 'em stay here;
Those that will follow Cassius, go with him;
And public reasons shall be rendered
Of Caesar's death.

Then follow me and listen, friends. Cassius, go part the crowds. Those who want to hear me speak, stay. Everyone else, go with Cassius. We will explain the reasons for Caesar's death.

First Citizen
I will hear Brutus speak.

I want to hear Brutus speak.

Second Citizen
I will hear Cassius; and compare their reasons,
When severally we hear them rendered.

I will listen to Cassius, so we can compare their reasons.

Exit Cassius with some of the Citizens. Brutus goes into the pulpit.

Third Citizen
The noble Brutus is ascended: silence!

The noble Brutus is ready. Silence!

Brutus
Be patient till the last.
Romans, countrymen, and lovers! Hear me for
my cause; and be silent, that you may hear:
believe me for mine honour, and have respect
to mine honor, that you may believe: censure
me in your wisdom; and awake your senses,
that you may the better judge. If there be any
in this assembly, any dear friend of Caesar's,
to him I say that Brutus' love to Caesar was no
less than his. If then that friend demand why
Brutus rose against Caesar, this is my answer,--
Not that I loved Caesar less, but that I loved
Rome more. Had you rather Caesar were living,
and die all slaves, than that Caesar were dead,

Please hear me out. Romans, countrymen, and lovers of Caesar, be quiet and listen to what I have to say. By my honor, believe me I loved Caesar as well as anyone. You are probably wondering why I rose against him. My reason is this, I loved Rome more. Ask yourself, if you had rather Caesar lived and die as a slave or had Caesar dead and live as free men. For his love, I wept for him. He was a fortunate man, and I rejoiced in his fortune. He was brave, and I honored him. But, he was ambitious, so I killed him. If there is anyone here whom I I have offended,

to live all freemen? As Caesar loved me, I weep
for him; as he was fortunate, I rejoice at it;
as he was valiant, I honour him; but, as he was
ambitious, I slew him. There is tears for his love;
joy for his fortune; honour for his valour; and
death for his ambition. Who is here so base that
would be a bondman? If any, speak; for him
have I offended. Who is here so rude that
would not be a Roman? If any, speak; for him
have I offended. Who is here so vile that will
not love his country? If any, speak; for him have
I offended. I pause for a reply.

then you are not a true Roman. Is there anyone who wants to speak against their country? I'm waiting.

All
None, Brutus, none.

None, Brutus, none.

Brutus
Then none have I offended. I have done no more
to Caesar than you shall do to Brutus.
The question of his death is enroll'd in the
Capitol, his glory not extenuated, wherein he
was worthy;, nor his offenses enforced,
for which he suffered death.

Then I haven't offended anyone. I have done no more to Caesar than you would do to me. Now you know the reasons for his death. He was a man worthy of glory, but his offences for which he died could not be tolerated.

Enter Antony and others with Caesar's body.

Here comes his body, mourned by Mark Antony,
who, though he had no hand in his death,
shall receive the benefit of his dying, a place in
the commonwealth; as which of you shall not?
With this I depart-- that, as I slew my best lover
for the good of Rome, I have the same dagger
for myself, when it shall please my country to
need my death.

Here comes his body, carried by Mark Antony, who had no part in his death but will benefit by taking a place in the senate. Is there anyone who objects? Now, I will depart saying I killed my best friend for the good of Rome. I hold the same dagger for myself, if it is for the good of Rome.

All
Live, Brutus! live, live!

Live, Brutus, live, live!

First Citizen
Bring him with triumph home unto his house.

Take him home with triumph.

Second Citizen
Give him a statue with his ancestors.

Erect a statue in his honor.

Third Citizen
Let him be Caesar.

Let him be Caesar.

Fourth Citizen

Caesar's better parts Shall be crown'd in Brutus.

Let him be crowned as an equal to Caesar.

First Citizen

We'll bring him to his house with shouts and clamours.

Let's carry him to his house and shout in victory.

Brutus

My countrymen,--

My countrymen...

Second Citizen

Peace! silence! Brutus speaks.

Be quiet! Silence! Brutus speaks.

First Citizen

Peace, ho!

Be quiet!

Brutus

Good countrymen, let me depart alone,
And, for my sake, stay here with Antony:
Do grace to Caesar's corpse, and grace his speech
Tending to Caesar's glory; which Mark Antony,
By our permission, is allow'd to make.
I do entreat you, not a man depart,
Save I alone, till Antony have spoke.

*My good countrymen, let me depart alone.
Stay here with Antony and honor Caesar's
body and listen to Antony's speech glorifying
Caesar. We are allowing Mark Antony to
speak, so I'm asking that you stay until Antony
is finished.*

Exit.

First Citizen

Stay, ho! and let us hear Mark Antony.

Stay everyone! Let's listen to Mark Antony.

Third Citizen

Let him go up into the public chair;
We'll hear him.--Noble Antony, go up.

*Let him go up to the podium.
We'll listen to him. Go on, noble Antony.*

Antony

For Brutus' sake, I am beholding to you.

For Brutus's sake, I will.

Goes into the pulpit.

Fourth Citizen

What does he say of Brutus?

What did he say about Brutus?

Third Citizen

He says, for Brutus' sake,
He finds himself beholding to us all.

*He said he was going to speak
for Brutus's sake and he owed it to us.*

Fourth Citizen
'Twere best he speak no harm of Brutus here.

He better not talk poorly about Brutus here.

First Caesar
This Caesar was a tyrant.

This Caesar was a tyrant.

Third Citizen
Nay, that's certain:
We are blest that Rome is rid of him.

That's for sure.
We are blessed that Rome is rid of him.

Second Citizen
Peace! let us hear what Antony can say.

Be quiet! Let's hear what Antony has to say.

Antony
You gentle Romans,--

Gentle Romans...

Citizens
Peace, ho! let us hear him.

Silence! Let's hear what he has to say.

Antony
Friends, Romans, countrymen, lend me your ears;
I come to bury Caesar, not to praise him.
The evil that men do lives after them;
The good is oft interred with their bones:
So let it be with Caesar. The noble Brutus
Hath told you Caesar was ambitious:
If it were so, it was a grievous fault;
And grievously hath Caesar answer'd it.
Here, under leave of Brutus and the rest,--
For Brutus is an honourable man;
So are they all, all honorable men,--
Come I to speak in Caesar's funeral.
He was my friend, faithful and just to me:
But Brutus says he was ambitious;
And Brutus is an honourable man.
He hath brought many captives home to Rome,
Whose ransoms did the general coffers fill:
Did this in Caesar seem ambitious?
When that the poor have cried, Caesar hath wept:
Ambition should be made of sterner stuff:
Yet Brutus says he was ambitious;
And Brutus is an honourable man.
You all did see that on the Lupercal
I thrice presented him a kingly crown,
Which he did thrice refuse: was this ambition?

Friends, Romans, and countrymen, listen to me. I have come to bury Caesar, not to praise him. The evil men do doesn't die with them, but the good is often buried with them. So, it will be true of Caesar. Brutus has told you of Caesar's ambition, and he is noble man. He has brought many prisoners home to Rome whose ransoms filled Rome's banks. Did Caesar seem ambitious when the he cried with the poor? Yet, Brutus said Caesar was ambitious, and Brutus is an honorable man. You all saw at the Lupercal I offered the crown to Caesar three times, and he refused each time. Did this seem like ambition? Yet, honorable Brutus said he was. I am not speaking to disagree with Brutus. I only speak of what I know. You all loved Caesar once and not without cause. Why aren't you mourning for him, now? Let you be judged as beasts without reason. Give me a moment; my heart is with Caesar. I must pause a moment until it comes back to me.

Yet Brutus says he was ambitious;
And, sure, he is an honourable man.
I speak not to disprove what Brutus spoke,
But here I am to speak what I do know.
You all did love him once,--not without cause:
What cause withholds you, then, to mourn for him?--
O judgment, thou art fled to brutish beasts,
And men have lost their reason!--Bear with me;
My heart is in the coffin there with Caesar,
And I must pause till it come back to me.

First Citizen
Methinks there is much reason in his sayings.

He makes a lot of sense.

Second Citizen
If thou consider rightly of the matter,
Caesar has had great wrong.

If you think about it, Caesar has been wronged.

Third Citizen
Has he not, masters?
I fear there will a worse come in his place.

I'm afraid someone worse than him will take his place.

Fourth Citizen
Mark'd ye his words? He would not take the crown;
Therefore 'tis certain he was not ambitious.

Listen to his words. He refused the crown; therefore, he was not ambitious.

First Citizen
If it be found so, some will dear abide it.

Some will agree to that.

Second Citizen
Poor soul! his eyes are red as fire with weeping.

Poor man! Look at Antony's eyes. They are as red as fire from crying.

Third Citizen
There's not a nobler man in Rome than Antony.

There is not a nobler man than Antony in all of Rome.

Fourth Citizen
Now mark him; he begins again to speak.

Listen! He is starting to speak again.

Antony
But yesterday the word of Caesar might
Have stood against the world: now lies he there,
And none so poor to do him reverence.
O masters, if I were disposed to stir
Your hearts and minds to mutiny and rage,
I should do Brutus wrong and Cassius wrong,
Who, you all know, are honourable men:

Yesterday, Caesar's words would have stood up against any in the world. Now, he lies there and no one is revering him. If I caused you men to be angry with honorable Brutus and Cassius, I would do them a wrong, as well as you and myself. Here's the will of Caesar, found in his study. If you could hear his last

I will not do them wrong; I rather choose
To wrong the dead, to wrong myself, and you,
Than I will wrong such honourable men.
But here's a parchment with the seal of Caesar,--
I found it in his closet,--'tis his will:
Let but the commons hear this testament,--
Which, pardon me, I do not mean to read,--
And they would go and kiss dead Caesar's wounds,
And dip their napkins in his sacred blood;
Yea, beg a hair of him for memory,
And, dying, mention it within their wills,
Bequeathing it as a rich legacy Unto their issue.

will and testament, you would kiss Caesar's wounds and beg for a hair to remember him by, which you would leave as a legacy in your will to pass down. I don't mean to read it though.

First Citizen
We'll hear the will: read it, Mark Antony.

We'll hear it. Read it Mark Antony!

All
The will, the will! We will hear Caesar's will.

The will! The will! We want to hear Caesar's will!

Antony
Have patience, gentle friends, I must not read it;
It is not meet you know how Caesar loved you.
You are not wood, you are not stones, but men;
And, being men, hearing the will of Caesar,
It will inflame you, it will make you mad.
'Tis good you know not that you are his heirs;
For if you should, O, what would come of it!

Gentle friends, be patient. I mustn't read it. You shouldn't know how much Caesar loved you. You are not made of wood or stone, and if you hear it, you will be angry. You should not hear that you were his heirs. I am scared to think what would happen next!

Fourth Citizen
Read the will! we'll hear it, Antony;
You shall read us the will,--Caesar's will!

Read the will. We want to hear it, Antony Read us the will of Caesar.

Antony
Will you be patient? will you stay awhile?
I have o'ershot myself to tell you of it:
I fear I wrong the honorable men
Whose daggers have stabb'd Caesar; I do fear it.

Will you be patient and stay a little longer? I shouldn't have told you about it. I am afraid I have caused harm to the honorable men who killed Caesar.

Fourth Citizen
They were traitors: honourable men!

Honorable men! They were traitors.

All
The will! The testament!

The will! The testament!

Second Citizen
They were villains, murderers.

They were villains! Murderers!

The will! read the will!

Read the will.

Antony
You will compel me, then, to read the will?
Then make a ring about the corpse of Caesar,
And let me show you him that made the will.
Shall I descend? and will you give me leave?

You will force to read the will?
Then, make a ring around Caesar's body,
and let me show you who wrote it.
Let me come down. Make way.

Several Citizens
Come down.

Come down.

Second Citizen
Descend.

Come down.

Third Citizen
You shall have leave.

We will make way.

Antony comes down.

Fourth Citizen
A ring! stand round.

Make a ring around the body.

First Citizen
Stand from the hearse, stand from the body.

Stand around the body.

SECOND CITIZEN
Room for Antony!--most noble Antony!

Room for Antony!--most noble Antony!

Antony
Nay, press not so upon me; stand far' off.

Give me some room. Stand back.

Several Citizens
Stand back; room! bear back.

Stand back. Make room.

Antony
If you have tears, prepare to shed them now.
You all do know this mantle: I remember
The first time ever Caesar put it on;
'Twas on a Summer's evening, in his tent,
That day he overcame the Nervii.
Look, in this place ran Cassius' dagger through:
See what a rent the envious Casca made:
Through this the well-beloved Brutus stabb'd;
And as he pluck'd his cursed steel away,
Mark how the blood of Caesar follow'd it,--
As rushing out of doors, to be resolved

If you have any tears, prepare to shed them
now. You all know this robe. I remember the
first time I saw him put it on. It was on a
summer's evening in his tent the day he
conquered Nervii. Look, this is where
Cassius's dagger went through his body.
See the whole Casca made. Here is where
the beloved Brutus stabbed him and pulled
his sword out. Look at how Caesar's blood
rushed out as if to ask for forgiveness.
Brutus, Caesar's angel, because you know

If Brutus so unkindly knock'd, or no;
For Brutus, as you know, was Caesar's angel:
Judge, O you gods, how dearly Caesar loved him!
This was the most unkindest cut of all;
For when the noble Caesar saw him stab,
Ingratitude, more strong than traitors' arms,
Quite vanquish'd him: then burst his mighty heart;
And, in his mantle muffling up his face,
Even at the base of Pompey's statua,
Which all the while ran blood, great Caesar fell.
O, what a fall was there, my countrymen!
Then I, and you, and all of us fell down,
Whilst bloody treason flourish'd over us.
O, now you weep; and, I perceive, you feel
The dint of pity: these are gracious drops.
Kind souls, what, weep you when you but behold
Our Caesar's vesture wounded? Look you here,
Here is himself, marr'd, as you see, with traitors.

how much Caesar loved him, caused the deadliest cut of all. The cut of ingratitude burst his heart. Great Caesar died at the base of Pompey's statue, where all his blood flowed out. I see you are touched and weep for him now, while you see what the traitors did to him.

First Citizen
O piteous spectacle!

What a pitiful sight!

Second Citizen
O noble Caesar!

Oh, noble Caesar!

Third Citizen
O woeful day!

What a terrible day!

Fourth Citizen
O traitors, villains!
First Citizen
O most bloody sight!

Oh, traitors! Villains!

This is the bloodiest sight!

Second Citizen
We will be revenged.
All
Revenge,--about,--seek,--burn,--fire,--kill,
--slay,--let not a traitor live!

We will seek revenge.

Revenge! Burn! Fire! Kill! Let not one traitor live!

Antony
Stay, countrymen.

Stop, countrymen.

First Citizen
Peace there! hear the noble Antony.

Be quiet! Listen to the noble Antony.

Second Citizen

We'll hear him, we'll follow him, we'll die with him.

Antony
Good friends, sweet friends, let me not stir you up
To such a sudden flood of mutiny.
They that have done this deed are honourable:
What private griefs they have, alas, I know not,
That made them do it; they're wise and honourable,
And will, no doubt, with reasons answer you.
I come not, friends, to steal away your hearts:
I am no orator, as Brutus is;
But, as you know me all, a plain blunt man,
That love my friend; and that they know full well
That gave me public leave to speak of him:
For I have neither wit, nor words, nor worth,
Action, nor utterance, nor the power of speech,
To stir men's blood: I only speak right on;
I tell you that which you yourselves do know;
Show you sweet Caesar's wounds, poor dumb mouths,
And bid them speak for me: but were I Brutus,
And Brutus Antony, there were an Antony
Would ruffle up your spirits, and put a tongue
In every wound of Caesar, that should move
The stones of Rome to rise and mutiny.

All
We'll mutiny.

First Citizen
We'll burn the house of Brutus.

Third Citizen
Away, then! come, seek the conspirators.

Antony
Yet hear me, countrymen; yet hear me speak.

All
Peace, ho! hear Antony; most noble Antony!

Antony
Why, friends, you go to do you know not what.
Wherein hath Caesar thus deserved your loves?
Alas, you know not; I must tell you then:

Let's hear him and follow him. We'll die with him.

Good friends, don't let me stir you up to the point of mutiny. Those who committed this act are honorable men with private grief. I don't know why they did it, but they are wise and honorable, and will give you their reasons. Don't let me change your hearts. I'm no orator like Brutus. I am just a plain man who loved his friend, and they allowed me to speak here today. I am not capable of stirring me to action. I'm only here to tell you what happened and show you Caesar's wounds, which speak for themselves. If I were Brutus, I might be able to cause a stir among you.

We'll mutiny.

We'll burn the house of Brutus.

Let's go! Seek the conspirators.

Listen to me countrymen. Hear me speak.

Shh! Listen to Antony! Most noble Antony!

You don't know what you are doing. You must know how Caesar deserved your love. You have forgotten about the will.

You have forgot the will I told you of.

All
Most true; the will!--let's stay, and hear the will.

True! The will! Let's stay and hear the will.

Antony
Here is the will, and under Caesar's seal.
To every Roman citizen he gives,
To every several man, seventy-five drachmas.

Here is the will bearing Caesar's seal. to every Roman citizen he gives seventy-five drachmas.

Second Citizen
Most noble Caesar!--we'll revenge his death.

Most noble Caesar! We'll revenge your death.

Third Citizen
O, royal Caesar!

Oh, royal Caesar!

Antony
Hear me with patience.

Listen to me. Be patient.

All
Peace, ho!

Be quiet!

Antony
Moreover, he hath left you all his walks,
His private arbors, and new-planted orchards,
On this side Tiber: he hath left them you,
And to your heirs forever; common pleasures,
To walk abroad, and recreate yourselves.
Here was a Caesar! when comes such another?

He also left you his land, including his trees and orchards on this side of the river Tiber. He has left them to you to enjoy, to walk among, and to pass along to your children. Here was a Caesar! I don't know if there will ever be another.

First Citizen
Never, never.--Come, away, away!
We'll burn his body in the holy place,
And with the brands fire the traitors' houses.
Take up the body.

Never, never! Let's go! We'll burn his body in the holy place, and carry the fire to the traitors' houses. Pick up the body.

Second Citizen
Go, fetch fire.

Go get the fire.

Third Citizen
Pluck down benches.

Get some wood. Take down the benches.

Fourth Citizen
Pluck down forms, windows, any thing.

Take down the window, the doors, anything.

Exit Citizens with the body.

Antony
Now let it work.--Mischief, thou art afoot,
Take thou what course thou wilt!--

*Now let come what may. Mischief, you are at
work. Let your course begin.*

Enter a Servant

How now, fellow?

How are you, fellow?

Servant
Sir, Octavius is already come to Rome.

Sir, Octavius is ready to come to Rome.

Antony
Where is he?

Where is he?

Servant
He and Lepidus are at Caesar's house.

He and Lepidus are at Caesar's house.

Antony
And thither will I straight to visit him:
He comes upon a wish. Fortune is merry,
And in this mood will give us any thing.

*I will go visit him. He is an answer to my
prayers. Fortune is on our side and will give
us whatever we want.*

Servant
I heard 'em say Brutus and Cassius
Are rid like madmen through the gates of Rome.

*I heard him say, Brutus and Cassius are like
madmen.*

Antony
Belike they had some notice of the people,
How I had moved them. Bring me to Octavius.

*The people are just as mad. Did you see how I
moved them? Bring me to Octavius.*

Exit.

Scene III: A street.

Enter Cinna the poet

Cinna the poet
I dreamt to-night that I did feast with Caesar,
And things unluckily charge my fantasy:
I have no will to wander forth of doors,
Yet something leads me forth.

*I dreamed tonight that I ate with Caesar,
And unlucky things ran through my fantasy:
I have no desire to enter the door,
Yet, something leads me forward.*

Enter Citizens.

First Citizen
What is your name?

What's your name?

Second Citizen
Whither are you going?

Where are you going?

Third Citizen
Where do you dwell?

Where do you live?

Fourth Citizen
Are you a married man or a bachelor?

Are you married or single?

Second Citizen
Answer every man directly.

Answer each man.

First Citizen
Ay, and briefly.

Yes, but brief.

Fourth Citizen
Ay, and wisely.

And choose your words wisely.

Third Citizen
Ay, and truly; you were best.

Yes and be honest.

Cinna the Poet
What is my name? Whither am I going?
Where do I dwell? Am I a married man or a
bachelor? Then, to answer every man directly
and briefly, wisely and truly.
Wisely I say I am a bachelor.

*What is my name? Where am I going?
Where do live? Am I married or single?
Well, to answer each of you directly and
briefly, wisely and honestly, then I say wisely,
"I am a bachelor."*

Second Citizen
That's as much as to say they are fools that marry;
you'll bear me a bang for that, I fear.
Proceed; directly.

Are you saying it is foolish to marry?
Careful, you are stepping on my toes. Go on.

Cinna the Poet
Directly, I am going to Caesar's funeral.

Honestly, I am going to Caesar's funeral.

First Citizen
As a friend, or an enemy?

Are you a friend or enemy?

Cinna the Poet
As a friend.

I am a friend.

Second Citizen
That matter is answered directly.

You answered that well.

Fourth Citizen
For your dwelling,--briefly.

And, where do you live? Be brief.

Cinna the Poet
Briefly, I dwell by the Capitol.

I live near the Capitol.

Third Citizen
Your name, sir, truly.

Tell us your name. Don't lie.

Cinna the Poet
Truly, my name is Cinna.

I am Cinna, honestly.

First Citizen
Tear him to pieces! he's a conspirator.

Tear him to pieces for he is one of the
conspirators.

Cinna the Poet
I am Cinna the poet, I am Cinna the poet.

I am Cinna the poet! I am Cinna the poet.

Fourth Citizen
Tear him for his bad verses,
tear him for his bad verses.

Kill him for his bad verses.
Kill him for his bad verses.

Cinna the Poet
I am not Cinna the conspirator.

I am not Cinna the conspirator.

Fourth Citizen
It is no matter, his name's Cinna;
pluck but his name out of his heart,
and turn him going.

It doesn't matter. His name's Cinna.
Pluck his name right out of his heart.

Third Citizen
Tear him, tear him! Come; brands, ho! firebrands.
To Brutus', to Cassius'; burn all. Some to Decius'
house, and some to Casca's, some to Ligarius':
away, go!

Exit.

Kill him! Kill him! Come, bring your fire.
Let's go to Brutus's, Cassius's, and burn
them all. Some of you go to Decius's house
and some got to Casca's and Ligarius's. Get
going!

Act IV

Scene I: A house in Rome.

Antony, Octavius, and Lepidus sit at a table.

Antony
These many then shall die; their names are prick'd.

These men will die. Their names are listed.

Octavius
Your brother too must die: consent you, Lepidus?

Your brother must die, too. Are you okay with that, Lepidus?

Lepidus
I do consent,--

I am.

Octavius
Prick him down, Antony.

Write his name down, too, Antony.

Lepidus
--Upon condition Publius shall not live,
Who is your sister's son, Mark Antony.

On one condition. Publius, your sister's son, must also die, Mark Antony.

Antony
He shall not live; look, with a spot I damn him.
But, Lepidus, go you to Caesar's house;
Fetch the will hither, and we shall determine
How to cut off some charge in legacies.

He shall not live. Look, I have written down his name to be damned. Lepidus, go to Caesar's house and get his will so we can figure out how to handle it.

Lepidus
What, shall I find you here?

Will you be here when I return?

Octavius
Or here, or at the Capitol.

Here or in the Capitol.

Exit Lepidus.

Antony
This is a slight unmeritable man,

This man is only fit to be sent on errands.

Meet to be sent on errands: is it fit,
The three-fold world divided, he should stand
One of the three to share it?

Octavius
So you thought him;
And took his voice who should be prick'd to die,
In our black sentence and proscription.

Antony
Octavius, I have seen more days than you:
And, though we lay these honors on this man,
To ease ourselves of divers slanderous loads,
He shall but bear them as the ass bears gold,
To groan and sweat under the business,
Either led or driven, as we point the way;
And having brought our treasure where we will,
Then take we down his load and turn him off,
Like to the empty ass, to shake his ears
And graze in commons.

Octavius
You may do your will;
But he's a tried and valiant soldier.

Antony
So is my horse, Octavius;and for that
I do appoint him store of provender:
It is a creature that I teach to fight,
To wind, to stop, to run directly on,
His corporal motion govern'd by my spirit.
And, in some taste, is Lepidus but so;
He must be taught, and train'd, and bid go forth:
A barren-spirited fellow; one that feeds
On objects, arts, and imitations,
Which, out of use and staled by other men,
Begin his fashion: do not talk of him
But as a property. And now, Octavius,
Listen great things. Brutus and Cassius
Are levying powers: we must straight make head;
Therefore let our alliance be combined,
Our best friends made, our means stretch'd;
And let us presently go sit in council,
How covert matters may be best disclosed,
And open perils surest answered.

Octavius

The world is about to be divided.
Should he be one of the three to share in this?

You thought he was when you started
to name the men who should die.

Octavius, I am older than you, and although,
we give this man the job to ease our burden,
he will bear it like a donkey bears gold.
He will groan and sweat. He will be led or
driven, and once we are finished with him,
we will take his load and turn him loose to
graze in the fields.

Do what you want,
but he's a honorable and courageous soldier.

So is my horse, Octavius, and for that
I give him food. He is someone who needs to
be taught and directed to go forward. He is
unspirited and feeds on stale traditions. Now,
Octavius, listen. Brutus and Cassius are
putting armies together. We must form an
alliance and begin to prepare.

Let us do so: for we are at the stake,
And bay'd about with many enemies;
And some that smile have in their hearts, I fear,
Millions of mischiefs.

Exit.

Let's get started for our lives are at stake.
We are surrounded by enemies with mischief
in their hearts who smile in our face.

Scene II: Camp near Sardis. Before Brutus's tent.

Drum. Enter Brutus, Lucilius, Lucius, and Soldiers. Titinius and Pindarus meet them.

Brutus
Stand, ho!

Stop!

Lucilius
Give the word, ho! and stand.

Tell everyone to stop!

Brutus
What now, Lucilius! is Cassius near?

What's going on, Lucilius? Is Cassius nearby?

Lucilius
He is at hand; and Pindarus is come
To do you salutation from his master.

*He's nearby, and Pindarus has come
to greet you on his behalf.*

Brutus
He greets me well.--Your master, Pindarus,
In his own change, or by ill officers,
Hath given me some worthy cause to wish
Things done, undone: but, if he be at hand,
I shall be satisfied.

*Pindarus, you are a good man, but your
master has either changed his mind or been
influenced by bad officers. I wish we hadn't
done some of the things we did. I need an
explanation.*

Pindarus
I do not doubt
But that my noble master will appear
Such as he is, full of regard and honour.

*I don't doubt that my noble master will show
up.*

Brutus
He is not doubted.--A word, Lucilius:
How he received you, let me be resolved.

*I don't doubt him. Lucilius, I need to ask
how Cassius received you.*

Lucilius
With courtesy and with respect enough;
But not with such familiar instances,
Nor with such free and friendly conference,
As he hath used of old.

*He treated me courteously and with respect,
but he wasn't friendly like he is usually.*

Brutus
Thou hast described
A hot friend cooling: ever note, Lucilius,
When love begins to sicken and decay,

*You have just described a friend in retreat.
Remember, Lucilius, when someone no longer
wants to be your friend,*

It useth an enforced ceremony.
There are no tricks in plain and simple faith;
But hollow men, like horses hot at hand,
Make gallant show and promise of their mettle;
But, when they should endure the bloody spur,
They fall their crests, and, like deceitful jades
Sink in the trial. Comes his army on?

they act as you have described. Hollow men are like showy horses. They look gallant, but when it's time to work, they disappear. Is his army coming?

Lucilius
They meant his night in Sard is to be quarter'd:
The greater part, the Horse in general,
Are come with Cassius.

They are in Sardis tonight to be dispersed. The largest is coming with Cassius.

Brutus
Hark! he is arrived.
March gently on to meet him.

Listen! He is here.

Low march within.

Let's go to meet him.

Enter Cassius and his men.

Cassius
Stand, ho!

Stop!

Brutus
Stand, ho! Speak the word along.

Stop! Tell the others.

First Soldier
Stand!

Stop!

Second Soldier
Stand!

Stop!

Third Soldier
Stand!

Stop!

Cassius
Most noble brother, you have done me wrong.

Most noble brother, you have done me wrong.

Brutus
Judge me, you gods! wrong I mine enemies?
And, if not so, how should I wrong a brother?

Let the gods judge me, if I have done you wrong. How I have I wronged you?

Cassius

Brutus, this sober form of yours hides wrongs;
And when you do them--

You may act like you haven't done anything, but you know you...

Brutus
Cassius, be content;
Speak your griefs softly, I do know you well.
Before the eyes of both our armies here,
Which should perceive nothing but love from us,
Let us not wrangle; bid them move away;
Then in my tent, Cassius, enlarge your griefs,
And I will give you audience.

Cassius, calm down. Tell me what's bothering you calmly. I know you very well. In front of both our armies, who should see nothing but love from us, let's not fight. Tell them to move on, and we'll go in my tent, so I can hear what you have to say.

Cassius
Pindarus,
Bid our commanders lead their charges off
A little from this ground.

Pindarus, tell the commanders to fall back.

Brutus
Lucilius, do you the like; and let no man
Come to our tent till we have done our
conference.—
Lucius and Titinius, guard our door.

Lucilius, you do the same, and don't let anyone come to my tent until we are done conferencing. Let Lucius and Titinius guard the door.

Exit.

Scene III: Brutus's tent.

Enter Brutus and Cassius

Cassius
That you have wrong'd me doth appear in this:
You have condemn'd and noted Lucius Pella
For taking bribes here of the Sardians;
Whereas my letters, praying on his side
Because I knew the man, were slighted off.

You wronged me when you condemned Lucius Pella for taking bribes from the Sardians. You ignored my letters on his behalf. I knew the man.

Brutus
You wrong'd yourself to write in such a case.

You were wrong to write those letters.

Cassius
In such a time as this it is not meet
That every nice offense should bear his comment.

In times like these, you shouldn't talk about others offences.

Brutus
Let me tell you, Cassius, you yourself
Are much condemn'd to have an itching palm,
To sell and mart your offices for gold
To undeservers.

You are one to talk when you sell your offices for to people who don't deserve them.

Cassius
I an itching palm!
You know that you are Brutus that speak this,
Or, by the gods, this speech were else your last.

*Are you calling me greedy?
If anybody else made such a claim against me, it would be their last.*

Brutus
The name of Cassius honors this corruption,
And chastisement doth therefore hide his head.

You use your name to cover up corruption.

Cassius
Chastisement!

Corruption!

Brutus
Remember March, the Ides of March remember:
Did not great Julius bleed for justice' sake?
What villain touch'd his body, that did stab,
And not for justice? What! shall one of us,
That struck the foremost man of all this world
But for supporting robbers,--shall we now

Remember in March, March 15th? Didn't the great Julius bleed for the sake of justice? Who stabbed him who was not seeking justice? Didn't we kill him for supporting robbers? Should we begin to do the same thing? I rather be a dog and howl at the moon than a

Contaminate our fingers with base bribes
And sell the mighty space of our large honours
For so much trash as may be grasped thus?
I had rather be a dog, and bay the moon,
Than such a Roman.

Cassius

Brutus, bay not me,
I'll not endure it: you forget yourself,
To hedge me in; I am a soldier, ay,
Older in practice, abler than yourself
To make conditions.

Brutus

Go to; you are not, Cassius.

Cassius

I am.

Brutus

I say you are not.

Cassius

Urge me no more, I shall forget myself;
Have mind upon your health, tempt me no farther.

Brutus

Away, slight man!

Cassius

Is't possible?

Brutus

Hear me, for I will speak.
Must I give way and room to your rash choler?
Shall I be frighted when a madman stares?

Cassius

O gods, ye gods! must I endure all this?

Brutus

All this? ay, more: fret till your proud heart break;
Go show your slaves how choleric you are,
And make your bondmen tremble. Must I budge?
Must I observe you? Must I stand and crouch
Under your testy humour? By the gods,

Roman like that.

Don't howl at me, Brutus. I won't take it. You've forgotten who you are talking to. I am a soldier, and much wiser than you, and more able to make things happen.

Go for it. You are not the Cassius, I used to know.

Oh, yes I am.

Well, I say you aren't.

You better stop, before I forget myself. Remember your health and don't tempt me.

Get out of here, little man!

Oh, yeah?

You better listen to what I'm saying. I will not be frightened by you.

Oh, gods! Must I endure this?

Yes! This and more! You can worry until your heart breaks. Why don't you go show your slaves how sick you are and try to make them scared? You won't do that to me. Do you expect me to cower in your presence?

You shall digest the venom of your spleen,
Though it do split you; for, from this day forth,
I'll use you for my mirth, yea, for my laughter,
When you are waspish.

You will die first. From this day forward, I will use you for comic relief.

Cassius
Is it come to this?

So this is what it's come to?

Brutus
You say you are a better soldier:
Let it appear so; make your vaunting true,
And it shall please me well: for mine own part,
I shall be glad to learn of abler men.

You say you are a better soldier. Prove it.

Cassius
You wrong me every way, you wrong me, Brutus.
I said, an elder soldier, not a better:
Did I say "better"?

How dare you! I said, "I was a wiser solder, not a better one."

Brutus
If you did, I care not.

Whatever.

Cassius
When Caesar lived, he durst not thus have moved
me.

Caesar never made me this angry when he lived.

Brutus
Peace, peace! you durst not so have tempted him.

You dared not treat him like this.

Cassius
I durst not?

I dared not!

Brutus
No.

No.

Cassius
What, durst not tempt him?

I dared not anger him!

Brutus
For your life you durst not.

You feared for your life, so you didn't dare.

Cassius
Do not presume too much upon my love;
I may do that I shall be sorry for.

You assume too much based on my love for you. You may force me to do something I will be sorry for.

Brutus
You have done that you should be sorry for.
There is no terror, Cassius, in your threats,
For I am arm'd so strong in honesty,
That they pass by me as the idle wind
Which I respect not. I did send to you
For certain sums of gold, which you denied me;--
For I can raise no money by vile means:
By Heaven, I had rather coin my heart,
And drop my blood for drachmas, than to wring
From the hard hands of peasants their vile trash
By any indirection:--I did send
To you for gold to pay my legions,
Which you denied me: was that done like Cassius?
Should I have answer'd Caius Cassius so?
When Marcus Brutus grows so covetous
To lock such rascal counters from his friends,
Be ready, gods, with all your thunderbolts,
Dash him to pieces!

You already have, and I am not afraid of your threats. Your idle threats go right by me. I sent you a request for money to pay for my army, and you denied me. Should I have resorted to steal from my friends to pay for my men, like you? May the gods curse me with their thunderbolts and tear me to pieces, if I do that!

Cassius
I denied you not.

I didn't deny you.

Brutus
You did.

Yes, you did.

Cassius
I did not. He was but a fool
That brought my answer back.
Brutus hath rived my heart:
A friend should bear his friend's infirmities,
But Brutus makes mine greater than they are.

I did not. My messenger must have been a fool when he delivered my answer. You have broken my heart. You should know me better than that. I am full of faults, but I would never do that to you.

Brutus
I do not, till you practise them on me.

I didn't think so, until you used them against me.

Cassius
You love me not.

You don't love me.

Brutus
I do not like your faults.

I don't like your faults.

Cassius
A friendly eye could never see such faults.

A friend would not see such faults.

Brutus

A flatterer's would not, though they do appear
As huge as high Olympus.

Cassius
Come, Antony and young Octavius, come,
Revenge yourselves alone on Cassius,
For Cassius is a-weary of the world;
Hated by one he loves; braved by his brother;
Check'd like a bondman; all his faults observed,
Set in a note-book, learn'd and conn'd by rote,
To cast into my teeth. O, I could weep
My spirit from mine eyes!--There is my dagger,
And here my naked breast; within, a heart
Dearer than Plutus' mine, richer than gold:
If that thou be'st a Roman, take it forth;
I, that denied thee gold, will give my heart:
Strike as thou didst at Caesar; for I know,
When thou didst hate him worst, thou lovedst him better
Than ever thou lovedst Cassius.

Brutus
Sheathe your dagger:
Be angry when you will, it shall have scope;
Do what you will, dishonor shall be humour.
O Cassius, you are yoked with a lamb
That carries anger as the flint bears fire;
Who, much enforced, shows a hasty spark,
And straight is cold again.

Cassius
Hath Cassius lived
To be but mirth and laughter to his Brutus,
When grief, and blood ill-temper'd, vexeth him?

Brutus
When I spoke that, I was ill-temper'd too.

Cassius
Do you confess so much? Give me your hand.

Brutus
And my heart too.

Cassius
O Brutus,--

I am your friend, not your slave, and your faults are as great as Mount Olympus.

Come, Antony and young Octavius are coming. You must fight them alone, because I am tired of this world. I am hated by someone I love. My faults have been listed and remembered to be thrown back in my face. Take this dagger and plunge it into my chest. Remove my heart, Roman, which is more valuable than Pluto's silver, if I denied you money. Kill me like you did Caesar, because I know you know you loved him better than me.

Put your dagger away. Be angry later, when it's time to be angry. You are like a lamb and I am like a flint with fire when it comes to carrying anger, here one minute and gone the next.

Am I just a cause to laugh at, Brutus, when you are angry?

I was angry when I said that.

You admit it then? Give me your hand.

Take my hand and my heart, too.

Oh, Brutus!

Brutus

What's the matter?

What's wrong?

Cassius

--Have not you love enough to bear with me,
When that rash humor which my mother gave me
Makes me forgetful?

Do you love me enough to forgive me when my faults are inherited from my mother?

Brutus

Yes, Cassius; and from henceforth,
When you are over-earnest with your Brutus,
He'll think your mother chides, and leave you so.

Yes, Cassius, and from now on when you are acting like this with me, I'll blame your mother.

Poet

[Within.]

Let me go in to see the generals:
There is some grudge between 'em; 'tis not meet
They be alone.

Let me in to see the generals. They shouldn't be alone.

Lucilius

[Within.]

You shall not come to them.

You can't go in.

Poet

[Within.]

Nothing but death shall stay me.

You'll have to kill me to stop me.

Enter Poet, followed by Lucilius, Titinius, and Lucius.

Cassius

How now! What's the matter?

Hey! What's the matter?

Poet

For shame, you generals! what do you mean?
Love, and be friends, as two such men should be;
For I have seen more years, I'm sure, than ye.

Shame on you generals for letting something come between such good friends.

Cassius

Ha, ha! How vilely doth this cynic rhyme!

Ha ha! This man is a terrible poet.

Brutus

Get you hence, sirrah; saucy fellow, hence!

Get out of here, you silly man!

Cassius

Bear with him, Brutus; 'tis his fashion.

Be patient with him, Brutus. That's just how

Brutus
I'll know his humor when he knows his time:
What should the wars do with these jigging
fools?--
Companion, hence!

he is.

*He should know when to be humorous.
What is he doing here during a war?*

Companion?

Cassius
Away, away, be gone!

You better go! Go on!

Exit Poet.

Brutus
Lucilius and Titinius, bid the commanders
Prepare to lodge their companies tonight.

*Lucilius and Titinius tell the commanders to
prepare their companies to stay tonight.*

Cassius
And come yourselves and bring Messala with you
Immediately to us.

*Go get Messala and come back to us
immediately.*

Brutus
Lucius, a bowl of wine!

Lucius, bring me a glass of wine.

Exit Lucius.

Cassius
I did not think you could have been so angry.

I didn't think you could get so angry.

Brutus
O Cassius, I am sick of many griefs.

Oh Cassius, I am sick with grief.

Cassius
Of your philosophy you make no use,
If you give place to accidental evils.

*I thought your philosophy was to not let things
like this bother you.*

Brutus
No man bears sorrow better. Portia is dead.

*I have more to be sorrowful about; Portia is
dead.*

Cassius
Ha! Portia!

No way! Portia!

Brutus
She is dead.
Cassius
How 'scaped I killing, when I cross'd you so?—
O insupportable and touching loss!—

She is dead.

*How did I escape being killed when I angered
you? What a terrible loss! Was she sick?*

Upon what sickness?

Brutus
Impatient of my absence,
And grief that young Octavius with Mark Antony
Have made themselves so strong;--for with her death
That tidings came;--with this she fell distract,
And, her attendants absent, swallow'd fire.

She was sick with worry about me being gone and the strong armies led by Octavius and Mark Antony, so she became depressed and she swallowed fire.

Cassius
And died so?

And it killed her?

Brutus
Even so.

Yes.

Cassius
O ye immortal gods!

Oh, immortal gods!

Re-enter Lucius, with wine and candle.

Brutus
Speak no more of her.--Give me a bowl of wine.—
In this I bury all unkindness, Cassius.

Let's not talk of her anymore. Give me the glass of wine. Let's drink and let bygones be bygones, Cassius.

Cassius
My heart is thirsty for that noble pledge.
Fill, Lucius, till the wine o'erswell the cup;
I cannot drink too much of Brutus' love.

I agree. Fill up the cup, Lucius. I can't get enough of Brutus's love.

Brutus
Come in, Titinius!--

Come in, Titinius!

Exit Lucius.

Re-enter Titinius with Messala.

Welcome, good Messala.—
Now sit we close about this taper here,
And call in question our necessities.

Welcome, Messala.
Sit with us and let's figure out what we need.

Cassius
Portia, art thou gone?

Oh Portia, are you gone?

Brutus
No more, I pray you.—
Messala, I have here received letters,
That young Octavius and Mark Antony
Come down upon us with a mighty power,
Bending their expedition toward Philippi.

Don't say anything else, please. Messala, I have letters here saying Octavius and Mark Antony are coming down on us with a huge army by way of Philippi.

Messala
Myself have letters of the selfsame tenour.

I have letters with the same message.

Brutus
With what addition?

Do they say anything else?

Messala
That by proscription and bills of outlawry
Octavius, Antony, and Lepidus
Have put to death an hundred Senators.

It says they have put to death a hundred senators.

Brutus
There in our letters do not well agree:
Mine speak of seventy Senators that died
By their proscriptions, Cicero being one.

My letters say about seventy senators were killed, one being Cicero.

Cassius
Cicero one!

Cicero was killed!

Messala
Cicero is dead,
And by that order of proscription.—
Had you your letters from your wife, my lord?

*He is dead.
Have you received your letters from your wife, my lord?*

Brutus
No, Messala.

No, Messala.

Messala
Nor nothing in your letters writ of her?

And, you haven't heard anything of her in your letters?

Brutus
Nothing, Messala.

Nothing, Messala.

Messala
That, methinks, is strange.

That's strange.

Brutus
Why ask you? hear you aught of her in yours?

Why? Have you heard something?

Messala
No, my lord.

No, my lord.

Brutus
Now, as you are a Roman, tell me true.

Tell me the truth, as a Roman.

Messala
Then like a Roman bear the truth I tell:
For certain she is dead, and by strange manner.

Then, like a Roman, she is dead, but by a strange manner.

Brutus
Why, farewell, Portia. We must die, Messala:
With meditating that she must die once,
I have the patience to endure it now.

Well, farewell, Portia. We must all die, Messala. I have dealt with it once. I have the patience to endure it now.

Messala
Even so great men great losses should endure.

Great men have to endure great losses.

Cassius
I have as much of this in art as you,
But yet my nature could not bear it so.

I don't think I could bear it.

Brutus
Well, to our work alive. What do you think
Of marching to Philippi presently?

Well, back to work. What do you think about marching to Philippi now?

Cassius
I do not think it good.

I don't think it's a good idea.

Brutus
Your reason?

Why not?

Cassius
This it is:
'Tis better that the enemy seek us;
So shall he waste his means, weary his soldiers,
Doing himself offense; whilst we, lying still,
Are full of rest, defense, and nimbleness.

Because I think the enemy should pursue us and wear out his soldiers. In the meantime, we sit and wait, full of rested men ready to fight.

Brutus
Good reasons must, of force, give place to better.
The people 'twixt Philippi and this ground
Do stand but in a forced affection;
For they have grudged us contribution:
The enemy, marching along by them,
By them shall make a fuller number up,

*That's a good reason, but there may be a better one to move us forward. Between here and Philippi,
they stand a chance of adding men to their regimen. If we meet them, we cut that chance off.*

Come on refresh'd, new-added, and encouraged;
From which advantage shall we cut him off,
If at Philippi we do face him there,
These people at our back.

Cassius
Hear me, good brother.

Listen, brother.

Brutus
Under your pardon. You must note besides,
That we have tried the utmost of our friends,
Our legions are brim-full, our cause is ripe:
The enemy increaseth every day;
We, at the height, are ready to decline.
There is a tide in the affairs of men
Which, taken at the flood, leads on to fortune;
Omitted, all the voyage of their life
Is bound in shallows and in miseries.
On such a full sea are we now afloat;
And we must take the current when it serves,
Or lose our ventures.

I beg your pardon, but you must remember our armies are full and ready. The enemy is increasing every day. We must act quickly while the time is right.

Cassius
Then, with your will, go on:
We'll along ourselves, and meet them at Philippi.

Then, we will go and meet them at Philippi.

Brutus
The deep of night is crept upon our talk,
And nature must obey necessity;
Which we will niggard with a little rest.
There is no more to say?

It's night now, so we better rest. Anything else?

Cassius
No more. Good night:
Early to-morrow will we rise, and hence.

No more. Goodnight.
We will begin early in the morning.

Enter Lucius.

Brutus
Lucius!—
My gown.--Farewell now, good Messala:--
Good night, Titinius:--noble, noble Cassius,
Good night, and good repose.

Lucius!
Bring me my gown.
Goodbye, Messala. Goodnight, Titinius.
Noble Cassius, goodnight and sleep well.

Exit Lucius.

Cassius
O my dear brother!
This was an ill beginning of the night.
Never come such division 'tween our souls!
Let it not, Brutus.

Oh, my dear brother.
We had a rough start tonight. May nothing
ever come between us, Brutus.

Brutus
Every thing is well.

All is well.

Cassius
Good night, my lord.

Goodnight, my lord.

Brutus
Good night, good brother.

Goodnight, my good brother.

Titinius and Messala
Good night, Lord Brutus.

Goodnight, Lord Brutus.

Brutus
Farewell, everyone.--

Farewell, everyone.

Exit all but Brutus.

Re-enter Lucius with the gown.

Give me the gown. Where is thy instrument?

Give me the gown. Where is your instrument?

Lucius
Here in the tent.

Here in the tent.

Brutus
What, thou speak'st drowsily:
Poor knave, I blame thee not, thou art o'er-watch'd.
Call Claudius and some other of my men;
I'll have them sleep on cushions in my tent.

You sound tired. Poor man, I don't blame you.
You have been overworked. Call Claudius
and some of the other men to sleep on
cushions in my tent.

Lucius
Varro and Claudius!

Varro and Claudius!

Enter Varro and Claudius.
Varro
Calls my lord?

You called, my lord?

Brutus

I pray you, sirs, lie in my tent and sleep;
It may be I shall raise you by-and-by
On business to my brother Cassius.

Do you mind, sirs, sleeping in here. I may wake up and need you to take a message to my brother, Cassius.

Varro
So please you, we will stand and watch your pleasure.

We will stand guard.

Brutus
I would not have it so; lie down, good sirs:
It may be I shall otherwise bethink me.—
Look, Lucius, here's the book I sought for so;
I put it in the pocket of my gown.

No, lie down. Look, Lucius, here's the book I was looking for. I put it in the pocket of my gown.

Varro and Claudius lie down.

Lucius
I was sure your lordship did not give it me.

I didn't think you gave it to me.

Brutus
Bear with me, good boy, I am much forgetful.
Canst thou hold up thy heavy eyes awhile,
And touch thy instrument a strain or two?

Sorry, boy, I am very forgetful. Can you stay awake a little longer and play some music?

Lucius
Ay, my lord, an't please you.

Yes, my lord, if it pleases you.

Brutus
It does, my boy:
I trouble thee too much, but thou art willing.

It does, my boy. I know I am a lot of trouble.

Lucius
It is my duty, sir.

It's my duty, sir.

Brutus
I should not urge thy duty past thy might;
I know young bloods look for a time of rest.

You need your rest, too. I shouldn't trouble you so much.

Lucius
I have slept, my lord, already.

I have already slept, my lord.

Brutus
It was well done; and thou shalt sleep again;
I will not hold thee long: if I do live,
I will be good to thee.--

I promise I won't keep you long, and if I do, I'll pay you back.

Music and song.

This is a sleepy tune.--O murderous Slumber,
Lay'st thou thy leaden mace upon my boy,
That plays thee music?--Gentle knave, good night;
I will not do thee so much wrong to wake thee:
If thou dost nod, thou breakst thy instrument;
I'll take it from thee; and, good boy, good night.—
Let me see, let me see; is not the leaf turn'd down
Where I left reading? Here it is, I think.

This is a sleepy tune. Oh, let the music help me sleep. You may go now. You might fall asleep on your instrument. Give it to me and have a good night. Let's see. Where did I leave off? Here is the page, I think.

Enter the Ghost of Caesar.

How ill this taper burns! Ha! who comes here?
I think it is the weakness of mine eyes
That shapes this monstrous apparition.
It comes upon me.--Art thou any thing?
Art thou some god, some angel, or some devil,
That makest my blood cold and my hair to stare?
Speak to me what thou art.

How weird this candle is burning! Who's there? My eyes must be weak; I think I see a ghost. Are you some god, or angel, or devil. You make my blood cold and my hair stand on end. Tell me what you are.

Ghost
Thy evil spirit, Brutus.

I am your evil spirit, Brutus.

Brutus
Why comest thou?

Why are you here?

Ghost
To tell thee thou shalt see me at Philippi.

To tell you I will be in Philippi.

Brutus
Well; then I shall see thee again?

Well, then I will see you again.

Ghost
Ay, at Philippi.

Yes, at Philippi.

Brutus
Why, I will see thee at Philippi, then.

Why will I see you at Philippi?

Exit Ghost.

Now I have taken heart, thou vanishest:
Ill spirit, I would hold more talk with thee.—
Boy! Lucius!--Varro! Claudius!
Sirs, awake!--Claudius!

Now, that I am curious, you have disappeared. Evil spirit, I would like to talk with you some more. Lucius! Varro! Claudius! Wake up! Claudius!

Lucius
The strings, my lord, are false.

The strings are not right, my lord.

Brutus
He thinks he still is at his instrument.--
Lucius, awake!

He thinks he's still playing his instrument.
Wake up, Lucius!

Lucius
My lord?

My lord?

Brutus
Didst thou dream, Lucius, that thou so criedst out?

Did you dream and cry out in your sleep,
Lucius?

Lucius
My lord, I do not know that I did cry.

I don't think so.

Brutus
Yes, that thou didst: didst thou see any thing?

You did. Did you see anything?

Lucius
Nothing, my lord.

Nothing, my lord.

Brutus
Sleep again, Lucius.--Sirrah Claudius!--
[To Varro.] Fellow thou, awake!

Go back to sleep, Lucius. Claudius!
[To Varro.] Are you awake?

Varro
My lord?

My lord?

Claudius
My lord?

My lord?

Brutus
Why did you so cry out, sirs, in your sleep?

Why did you all cry out in your sleep?

Varro and Claudius
Did we, my lord?

Did we, my lord?

Brutus
Ay: saw you any thing?

Yes, did you see anything?

Varro
No, my lord, I saw nothing.

No, I didn't.

Claudius
Nor I, my lord.

Me either.

Brutus
Go and commend me to my brother Cassius;
Bid him set on his powers betimes before,
And we will follow.

Varro and Claudius
It shall be done, my lord.

Exit.

Go tell Cassius, to set out first thing and we will follow him.

We will, my lord.

Act V

Scene I: The plains of Philippi.

Enter Octavius, Antony, and their army.

Octavius
Now, Antony, our hopes are answered.
You said the enemy would not come down,
But keep the hills and upper regions:
It proves not so; their battles are at hand:
They mean to warn us at Philippi here,
Answering before we do demand of them.

*Now, Antony, our hopes are answered.
You thought the enemy wouldn't come to us,
but stay in the hills. Yet, here they are to meet
us.*

Antony
Tut, I am in their bosoms, and I know
Wherefore they do it: they could be content
To visit other places; and come down
With fearful bravery, thinking by this face
To fasten in our thoughts that they have courage;
But 'tis not so.

*I know them, and I know what they are up to.
They want us to think they are brave, but I
know better.*

Enter a Messenger.

Messenger
Prepare you, generals:
The enemy comes on in gallant show;
Their bloody sign of battle is hung out,
And something to be done immediately.

*Get ready, generals, the enemy is coming.
Their battle sign is out and something needs
to be done immediately.*

Antony
Octavius, lead your battle softly on,
Upon the left hand of the even field.

*Octavius, lead your men on the left side of the
field.*

Octavius
Upon the right hand I; keep thou the left.

I'll take the right. You take the left.

Antony

Why do you cross me in this exigent?

Why do you disagree with me in this dire hour?

Octavius
I do not cross you; but I will do so.

I'm not disagreeing with you, but I will.

March.

Drum. Enter Brutus, Cassius, and their armies. Lucilius, Titinius, Messalus, and others.

Brutus
They stand, and would have parley.

They stand and are ready to fight.

Cassius
Stand fast, Titinius: we must out and talk.

Stay here, Titinius. We must ride out and talk.

Octavius
Mark Antony, shall we give sign of battle?

Mark Antony, shall we give sign of battle?

Antony
No, Caesar, we will answer on their charge.
Make forth; the generals would have some words.

No, Caesar, we wait until they charge. Go forward. The generals want to talk.

Octavius
Stir not until the signal.

Don't do anything until I give you the signal.

Brutus
Words before blows: is it so, countrymen?

Words before blows. So, that's how it's going to be, countrymen.

Octavius
Not that we love words better, as you do.

We don't love words like you do.

Brutus
Good words are better than bad strokes, Octavius.

Good words are better than bad fighting, Octavius.

Antony
In your bad strokes, Brutus, you give good words:
Witness the hole you made in Caesar's heart,
Crying, "Long live! Hail, Caesar!"

You have good words for your bad deeds. Weren't you crying out, "Hail, Caesar," when you were stabbing him?

Cassius
Antony,
The posture of your blows are yet unknown;
But for your words, they rob the Hybla bees,
And leave them honeyless.

Antony, we don't know how well you fight, but your words drip with honey.

Antony

Not stingless too.

They don't sting, though.

Brutus
O, yes, and soundless too,
For you have stol'n their buzzing, Antony,
And very wisely threat before you sting.

Your words are not soundless, either.
They are very effective, Antony, warning your
enemy before you fight.

Antony
Villains, you did not so when your vile daggers
Hack'd one another in the sides of Caesar:
You show'd your teeth like apes, and fawn'd
like hounds,
And bow'd like bondmen, kissing Caesar's feet;
Whilst damned Casca, like a cur, behind
Struck Caesar on the neck. O flatterers!

That's better than what you did when you
acted like beasts and killed Caesar, stabbing
him in his sides, while Casca struck from
behind, you flatterers.

behind, you flatterers.

Cassius
Flatterers!--Now, Brutus, thank yourself:
This tongue had not offended so to-day,
If Cassius might have ruled.

Flatterers! We wouldn't be here were I the
ruler.

Octavius
Come, come, the cause:
if arguing makes us sweat,
The proof of it will turn to redder drops.
Look,--
I draw a sword against conspirators:
When think you that the sword goes up again?
Never, till Caesar's three and thirty wounds
Be well avenged; or till another Caesar
Have added slaughter to the sword of traitors.

Come on, get to the point. We aren't here
to argue. I draw my sword against
conspirators and keep it up until Caesar's
death is avenged, or until I have been
killed by the same traitors.

Brutus
Caesar, thou canst not die by traitors' hands,
Unless thou bring'st them with thee.

You aren't going to die at the hands of a
traitor, unless you kill yourself.

Octavius
So I hope;
I was not born to die on Brutus' sword.

That's my hope.
I was not born to die on Brutus's sword.

Brutus
O, if thou wert the noblest of thy strain,
Young man, thou couldst not die more honourably.

You couldn't die a more honorable death.

Cassius
A peevish school boy, worthless of such honour,
Join'd with a masker and a reveller!

You are just a school boy and not worthy of such an honor.

Antony
Old Cassius still!

There's the old Cassius!

Octavius
Come, Antony; away!—
Defiance, traitors, hurl we in your teeth:
If you dare fight today, come to the field;
If not, when you have stomachs.

Come on, Antony. Let's go! Traitors, if you dare to fight today, come to the field. If not, come when you have the stomachs for it.

Exit Octavius, Antony, and their armies.

Cassius
Why, now, blow wind, swell billow, and swim bark!
The storm is up, and all is on the hazard.

Why now are we having a storm?

Brutus
Ho, Lucilius! Hark, a word with you.

Hey, Lucilius! Listen, I need a word with you.

Lucilius
Standing forward.
My lord?

I'm listening.

CASSIUS
Messala,--

Messala,--

MESSALA
What says my General?

What says my General?

Cassius
Messala,
This is my birth-day; as this very day
Was Cassius born. Give me thy hand, Messala:
Be thou my witness that against my will,
As Pompey was, am I compell'd to set
Upon one battle all our liberties.
You know that I held Epicurus strong,
And his opinion: now I change my mind,
And partly credit things that do presage.
Coming from Sardis, on our former ensign

Messala, this is my birthday. Give me your hand and be my witness that I am here against my will. I am going to set all of our freedom on the line. You know that believed in Epicurus, but now I have changed my mind. On the way from Sardis, I saw two mighty eagles fall and feed from our soldiers' hands. They are gone, now, and ravens and crows circle us like we are about to be prey.

Two mighty eagles fell; and there they perch'd,
Gorging and feeding from our soldiers' hands;
Who to Philippi here consorted us:
This morning are they fled away and gone;
And in their steads do ravens, crows, and kites
Fly o'er our heads and downward look on us,
As we were sickly prey: their shadows seem
A canopy most fatal, under which
Our army lies, ready to give up the ghost.

We seem ready to die.

Messala
Believe not so.

I don't think so.

Cassius
I but believe it partly;
For I am fresh of spirit, and resolved
To meet all perils very constantly.

I believe it partly, because I am ready.

Brutus
Even so, Lucilius.

Even so, Lucilius.

Cassius
Now, most noble Brutus,
The gods to-day stand friendly, that we may,
Lovers in peace, lead on our days to age!
But, since th' affairs of men rest still incertain,
Let's reason with the worst that may befall.
If we do lose this battle, then is this
The very last time we shall speak together:
What are you then determined to do?

Now, most noble Brutus, the gods are going to be friendly today so we lovers of peace may live to a ripe old age. But, since we are still unsure how this is going to turn out let's just say we lose today. What are you going to do then?

Brutus
Even by the rule of that philosophy
By which I did blame Cato for the death
Which he did give himself;--I know not how,
But I do find it cowardly and vile,
For fear of what might fall, so to prevent
The time of life;--arming myself with patience
To stay the providence of some high powers
That govern us below.

I am going to stay the course with patience, unlike Cato who killed himself for fear of the unknown.

Cassius
Then, if we lose this battle,
You are contented to be led in triumph
Thorough the streets of Rome?
Brutus

Then, if we lose, you are going to be content to be led through the streets of Rome?

No, Cassius, no: think not, thou noble Roman,
That ever Brutus will go bound to Rome;
He bears too great a mind. But this same day
Must end that work the Ides of March begun;
And whether we shall meet again I know not.
Therefore our everlasting farewell take:
For ever, and for ever, farewell, Cassius!
If we do meet again, why, we shall smile;
If not, why, then this parting was well made.

Cassius
For ever and for ever farewell, Brutus!
If we do meet again, we'll smile indeed;
If not, 'tis true this parting was well made.

Brutus
Why then, lead on. O, that a man might know
The end of this day's business ere it come!
But it sufficeth that the day will end,
And then the end is known.--Come, ho! away!

Exit.

No, Cassius, I don't think so. Any Roman who thinks I will go into Rome in handcuffs thinks too much of himself. Today, we will finish what was started on March 15th. I don't know if we will meet again, so let's say our goodbyes. Farewell, Cassius! If we do meet again, let's smile, and know we parted well.

If we meet again, Brutus, we will smile, indeed. If not, we did part well.

Well, then, let's go. I wish I knew what is about to happen, but the day will end all the same and then, I'll know. Let's go!

Scene II: The same field of battle.

Alarm. Enter Brutus and Messala.

Brutus
Ride, ride, Messala, ride, and give these bills
Unto the legions on the other side:
Let them set on at once; for I perceive
But cold demeanor in Octavius' wing,
And sudden push gives them the overthrow.
Ride, ride, Messala: let them all come down.

Exit.

*Ride, ride, Messala, and give these orders
to the men on the other side.
Loud alarm.
Let them start at once, because I because
I believe Octavius's men are not ready.
Hurry, Messala, ride. Let them all come down.*

Scene III: Another part of the field.

Alarms. Enter Cassius and Titinius.

Cassius
O, look, Titinius, look, the villains fly!
Myself have to mine own turn'd enemy:
This ensign here of mine was turning back;
I slew the coward, and did take it from him.

*Oh, look, Titinius. Look, the enemy is fleeing!
One of my men tried to turn back, but I killed
him.*

Titinius
O Cassius, Brutus gave the word too early;
Who, having some advantage on Octavius,
Took it too eagerly: his soldiers fell to spoil,
Whilst we by Antony are all enclosed.

*Oh, Cassius, Brutus gave the word too early.
He thought he had advantage over Octavius,
but he was too eager. His soldiers have
started looting, and we're surrounded by
Antony.*

Pindarus
Fly further off, my lord, fly further off;
Mark Antony is in your tents, my lord:
Fly, therefore, noble Cassius, fly far' off.

*You must flee, my lord, go away.
Mark Antony is in your tents, my lord.
You must leave.*

Cassius
This hill is far enough.--Look, look, Titinius;
Are those my tents where I perceive the fire?

*I will go to the hills. Are those my tents over
there where I see fire?*

Titinius
They are, my lord.

They are, my lord.

Cassius
Titinius, if thou lovest me,
Mount thou my horse and hide thy spurs in him,
Till he have brought thee up to yonder troops
And here again; that I may rest assured
Whether yond troops are friend or enemy.

*Titinius, if you love me, get on my horse and
spur him until he has taken you up to the
troops and back again, so I may know if
the troops are friend or enemy.*

Titinius
I will be here again, even with a thought.

I will be right back.

Exit.

Cassius
Go, Pindarus, get higher on that hill:
My sight was ever thick: regard Titinius,

*Pindarus, get higher on that hill and watch
Titinius. Tell me what you see on the*

And tell me what thou notest about the field.--

Pindarus ascends the hill.

This day I breathed first: time is come round,
And where I did begin, there shall I end;
My life is run his compass.--Sirrah, what news?

Pindarus
Above.
O my lord!

Cassius
What news?

Pindarus
Above.
Titinius is enclosed round about
With horsemen, that make to him on the spur:
Yet he spurs on. Now they are almost on him.—
Now, Titinius!--Now some 'light. O, he 'lights too:
He's ta'en; [Shout.] and, hark! they shout for joy.

Shout!

They are shouting for joy.

Cassius
Come down; behold no more.—
O, coward that I am, to live so long,
To see my best friend ta'en before my face!

Pindarus descends.
Come hither, sirrah:
In Parthia did I take thee prisoner;
And then I swore thee, saving of thy life,
That whatsoever I did bid thee do,
Thou shouldst attempt it.
Come now, keep thine oath;
Now be a freeman; and with this good sword,
That ran through Caesar's bowels, search this
bosom.
Stand not to answer: here, take thou the hilts;
And when my face is cover'd, as 'tis now,
Guide thou the sword.--Caesar, thou art revenged,
Even with the sword that kill'd thee.

battlefield.

*This is the first and last day I will breathe.
My life has run its course. What news, sir?*

Oh, my lord!

What is it?

*Titinius is surrounded by men who are
chasing him. They are almost on him. Now,
Titinius is getting down. They have taken him.*

*Come down. Don't look anymore.
Oh, I am such a coward to watch my best
friend be taken before my eyes!*

*Come here, sir. I took you prisoner in Parthia,
and I swore after I saved your life you had to
do whatever I asked. It's time to keep that
oath. Be a freeman and with this sword that
killed Caesar, stab me in the heart. Don't
stand there. Take it, and when my face is
covered, do it.*

Pindarus stabs him.

*Caesar, you are revenged with the sword
that killed you.*

Dies.

Pindarus
So, I am free, yet would not so have been,
Durst I have done my will.--O Cassius!
Far from this country Pindarus shall run,
Where never Roman shall take note of him.

Exit.

Re-enter Titinius with Messala.

Messala
It is but change, Titinius; for Octavius
Is overthrown by noble Brutus' power,
As Cassius' legions are by Antony.

Titinius
These tidings would well comfort Cassius.

Messala
Where did you leave him?

Titinius
All disconsolate,
With Pindarus his bondman, on this hill.

Messala
Is not that he that lies upon the ground?

Titinius
He lies not like the living. O my heart!

Messala
Is not that he?

Titinius
No, this was he, Messala,
But Cassius is no more.--O setting Sun,
As in thy red rays thou dost sink to night,
So in his red blood Cassius' day is set,
The sun of Rome is set! Our day is gone;
Clouds, dews, and dangers come; our deeds are
done!
Mistrust of my success hath done this deed.

So, I am free, but I wouldn't be if I had way. Oh, Cassius, I am going to run far from here where no Roman can find me.

Octavius is overthrown and Antony took Cassius's men.

Cassius will be comforted by this message.

Where did you leave him?

He was here on this hill with his slave, Pindarus.

Isn't that him on the ground?

He doesn't look alive. Oh, my heart!

Isn't that him?

Yes, this is him, Messala. Cassius's life is over like the setting sun, spreading its red light over the earth. Our day is gone and our deeds are done. He didn't believe I would make it.

Messala

Mistrust of good success hath done this deed.
O hateful Error, Melancholy's child!
Why dost thou show to the apt thoughts of men
The things that are not? O Error, soon conceived,
Thou never comest unto a happy birth,
But kill'st the mother that engender'd thee!

He didn't think you would succeed and his error has cost him his life. Why do men always imagine the worst?

Titinius

What, Pindarus! where art thou, Pindarus?

Where is Pindarus? Pindarus!

Messala

Seek him, Titinius, whilst I go to meet
The noble Brutus, thrusting this report
Into his ears: I may say, thrusting it;
For piercing steel and darts envenomed
Shall be as welcome to the ears of Brutus
As tidings of this sight.

Look for him, Titinius, while I go meet Brutus and tell him what has happened. Brutus is not going to like hearing this.

Titinius

Hie you, Messala,
And I will seek for Pindarus the while.--

Hurry, Messala, and I will look for Pindarus.

Exit Messala.

Why didst thou send me forth, brave Cassius?
Did I not meet thy friends? And did not they
Put on my brows this wreath of victory,
And bid me give it thee?
Didst thou not hear their shouts?
Alas, thou hast misconstrued every thing!
But, hold thee, take this garland on thy brow;
Thy Brutus bid me give it thee, and I
Will do his bidding.--Brutus, come apace,
And see how I regarded Caius Cassius.—
By your leave, gods: this is a Roman's part:
Come, Cassius' sword, and find Titinius' heart.

Why did you send me, brave Cassius? Didn't I meet your friends who gave me this wreath of victory to give to you? Didn't you hear the cheering? You misunderstood everything! But, take this wreath and wear it like Brutus wanted, so he can see I followed orders. Now, by the gods, I am taking your sword to find my heart.

Kills himself.

Alarms. Re-enter Messala with Brutus, Cato, Strato, Volumnius and Lucilius.

Brutus

Where, where, Messala, doth his body lie?

Where, Messala, is his body?

Messala
Lo, yonder, and Titinius mourning it.

Over there, with Titinius mourning over it.

Brutus
Titinius' face is upward.

Titinius is lying face up.

Cato
He is slain.

He is dead.

Brutus
O Julius Caesar, thou art mighty yet!
Thy spirit walks abroad, and turns our swords
In our own proper entrails.

*Oh, Julius Caesar, you are still mighty!
Your spirit walks around and turns our
swords against us.*

Low alarms.

Cato
Brave Titinius!
Look whether he have not crown'd dead Cassius!

Brave Titinius! See if he crowned Cassius.

Brutus
Are yet two Romans living such as these?—
The last of all the Romans, fare thee well!
It is impossible that ever Rome
Should breed thy fellow.—
Friends, I owe more tears
To this dead man than you shall see me pay.—
I shall find time, Cassius, I shall find time.—
Come therefore, and to Thassos send his body:
His funerals shall not be in our camp,
Lest it discomfort us.--Lucilius, come;--
And come, young Cato;--let us to the field.—
Labeo and Flavius, set our battles on:--
'Tis three o'clock; and Romans, yet ere night
We shall try fortune in a second fight.

*Are there two Romans alive like these?
They were the last of their kind. Friends,
I should cry, but I will not. Cassius, I will
find time to mourn you. Send his body to
Thasos for the funeral. We don't want to
have it in the camp. Lucilius and young Cato,
let's go back to the battlefield. Laveo and
Flavius get ready to fight. We will try a
second time to triumph.*

Exit.

Scene IV: Another part of the field.

Alarm. Enter fighting soldiers of both armies, then Brutus, Cato, Lucilius, and others.

Brutus
Yet, countrymen, O, yet hold up your heads!

Hold up your heads, countrymen! Don't give up!

Cato
What bastard doth not? Who will go with me?
I will proclaim my name about the field:--
I am the son of Marcus Cato, ho!
A foe to tyrants, and my country's friend;
I am the son of Marcus Cato, ho!

What bastard is not? Who will go with me? I will proclaim my name about the field. I am the son of Marcus Cato, a foe to tyrants and a friend to Rome. I am the son of Marcus Cato!

Brutus
And I am Brutus, Marcus Brutus, I;
Brutus, my country's friend; know me for Brutus!

And I am Brutus, Marcus Brutus. I am my country's friend. You know me!

Exit.

Lucilius
O young and noble Cato, art thou down?
Why, now thou diest as bravely as Titinius;
And mayst be honour'd, being Cato's son.

Oh, young and noble Cato, are you hurt? You have died as bravely as Titinius and will be honored as Cato's son.

First Soldier
Yield, or thou diest.

We must give up or die.

Lucilius
Only I yield to die:
There is so much that thou wilt kill me straight;
[Offering money.]
Kill Brutus, and be honour'd in his death.

I will only give up to death.
[Offering money.]
Kill Brutus, and be honored for his death.

First Soldier
We must not. A noble prisoner!

We can't. He is a noble prisoner!

Second Soldier
Room, ho! Tell Antony, Brutus is ta'en.

Make way! Tell Antony, Brutus has been captured.

First Soldier
I'll tell the news. Here comes the General.--

I'll tell him. Here comes the general.

Enter Antony.
Brutus is ta'en, Brutus is ta'en, my lord.

Antony
Where is he?

Lucilius
Safe, Antony; Brutus is safe enough:
I dare assure thee that no enemy
Shall ever take alive the noble Brutus:
The gods defend him from so great a shame!
When you do find him, or alive or dead,
He will be found like Brutus, like himself.

Antony
This is not Brutus, friend; but, I assure you,
A prize no less in worth. Keep this man safe,
Give him all kindness; I had rather have
Such men my friends than enemies. Go on,
And see whether Brutus be alive or dead;
And bring us word unto Octavius' tent
How everything is chanced.

Exit.

Brutus is ta'en, Brutus is ta'en, my lord.

Where is he?

*He is safe enough, Antony. I assure you
no enemy will take him alive. The gods
defend him from such a great shame!
When you do find him, he will be Brutus,
alive or dead.*

*This is not Brutus, friend, but I assure you it is
a prize, nevertheless. Keep this man safe.
Treat him with kindness. I had rather have
such men as my friends than my enemies.
Go on, and see if Brutus is alive or dead,
and come tell us in Octavius's tent.*

Scene V: Another part of the field.

Enter Brutus, Dardanius, Clitus, Strato, and Volumnius.

Brutus
Come, poor remains of friends, rest on this rock.   *Come on, friends. Let's rest on this rock.*

Clitus
Statilius show'd the torch-light; but, my lord,   *Statilius showed the torch was lit, but he never*
He came not back: he is or ta'en or slain.   *came back. He is either captured or dead.*

Brutus
Sit thee down, Clitus: slaying is the word;   *Sit down, Clitus. He is probably dead. Listen.*
It is a deed in fashion. Hark thee, Clitus.

Whispers.

Clitus
What, I, my lord? No, not for all the world.   *No, not me lord. Not for all of the world.*

Brutus
Peace then! no words.   *Be quiet, then.*

Clitus
I'll rather kill myself.   *I'd rather kill myself.*

Brutus
Hark thee, Dardanius.   *Listen, Dardanius.*

Whispers.

Dardanius
Shall I do such a deed?   *Would I do such a deed?*

Clitus
O Dardanius!   *Oh, Dardanius!*

Dardanius
O Clitus!   *Oh, Clitus!*

Clitus
What ill request did Brutus make to thee?   *What did Brutus ask of you?*

Dardanius

To kill him, Clitus. Look, he meditates.

He wants me to kill him. Look, he's thinking about it.

Clitus

Now is that noble vessel full of grief,
That it runs over even at his eyes.

He is so full of grief, it is running over in his eyes.

Brutus

Come hither, good Volumnius; list a word.

Come here, Volumnius. I need a word with you.

Volumnius

What says my lord?

What do you need, my lord?

Brutus

Why, this, Volumnius:
The ghost of Caesar hath appear'd to me
Two several times by night; at Sardis once,
And this last night here in Philippi fields:
I know my hour is come.

The ghost of Caesar has appeared to me twice by night, once in Sardis and last night in Philippi. I know my time has come.

Volumnius

Not so, my lord.

You don't know that, my lord.

Brutus

Nay I am sure it is, Volumnius.
Thou seest the world, Volumnius, how it goes;
Our enemies have beat us to the pit:

No, I am sure of it, Volumnius. Our enemies have beaten us. I know what's coming next.

Low alarms.

It is more worthy to leap in ourselves
Than tarry till they push us. Good Volumnius,
Thou know'st that we two went to school together;
Even for that our love of old, I pr'ythee,
Hold thou my sword-hilts, whilst I run on it.

It is better to off ourselves than have them do it. Volumnius, you know we went to school together. We go back a long way. Please, hold my sword, so I may run into it.

Volumnius

That's not an office for a friend, my lord.

That's not something a friend can do, my lord.

Alarm.

Clitus

Fly, fly, my lord! there is no tarrying here.

Run, run, my lord. You can't sit here.

Brutus

Farewell to you;--and you;--and you, Volumnius.— *Farewell my friends. Goodbye, Strato.*
Strato, thou hast been all this while asleep; *My heart is full of joy that in all of my life,*
Farewell to thee too, Strato.--Countrymen, *I never met an untrue man. I will have triumph*
My heart doth joy, that yet in all my life *greater than Octavius and Mark Antony*
I found no man but he was true to me. *today. So, goodbye once and for all.*
I shall have glory by this losing day, *It's my time to rest.*
More than Octavius and Mark Antony
By this vile conquest shall attain unto.
So, fare you well at once; for Brutus' tongue
Hath almost ended his life's history:
Night hangs upon mine eyes; my bones would rest
That have but labour'd to attain this hour.

Alarm. Cries to run from within.

Clitus

Fly, my lord, fly!   *Run, my lord, run.*

Brutus

Hence! I will follow.--   *Go. I will follow.*

Exit Clitus, Dardanius, and Volumnius.

I pr'ythee, Strato, stay thou by thy lord: *I pray you will help me, Strato.*
Thou art a fellow of a good respect;   *You are respectful fellow, and your life has*
Thy life hath had some smack of honor in it: *been honorable. Hold my sword and turn your*
Hold, then, my sword, and turn away thy face,   *eyes away. Will you, Strato?*
While I do run upon it. Wilt thou, Strato?

Strato

Give me your hand first: fare you well, my lord. *Give me your hand first. Goodbye, my lord.*

Brutus

Farewell, good Strato.--Caesar, now be still: *Goodbye, Strato.*
I kill'd not thee with half so good a will.   *Caesar, you may rest. I wanted to kill myself*
                                                 more than you.

Runs on his sword.

Dies.

Alarm. Retreat. Enter Octavius, Antony, Messala, Lucilius, and the army.

Octavius

What man is that?   *Who is that man?*

Messala

My master's man.--Strato, where is thy master?

Strato
Free from the bondage you are in, Messala:
The conquerors can but make a fire of him;
For Brutus only overcame himself,
And no man else hath honour by his death.

Lucilius
So Brutus should be found.--I thank thee, Brutus,
That thou hast proved Lucilius' saying true.

Octavius
All that served Brutus, I will entertain them.—
Fellow, wilt thou bestow thy time with me?

Strato
Ay, if Messala will prefer me to you.

Octavius
Do so, good Messala.

Messala
How died my master, Strato?

Strato
I held the sword, and he did run on it.

Messala
Octavius, then take him to follow thee,
That did the latest service to my master.

Antony
This was the noblest Roman of them all:
All the conspirators, save only he,
Did that they did in envy of great Caesar;
He only, in a general-honest thought
And common good to all, made one of them.
His life was gentle; and the elements
So mix'd in him that Nature might stand up
And say to all the world, "This was a man!"

Octavius
According to his virtue let us use him
With all respect and rites of burial.
Within my tent his bones to-night shall lie,

My master's man. Strato, where is your master?

He is free from the bondage you are in, Messala. The conquerors can burn him, but they can't kill him, so no man can claim honor by his death.

So, Brutus should be found. Thank you, Brutus, for proving me right.

All that served Brutus will be entertained. Will you give me your time?

Yes, if Messala will prefer me to you.

Do so, Messala.

How did my master die, Strato?

I held the sword and he ran upon it.

You may have him, Octavius, for his service to my master.

This was the noblest Roman of them all. All the conspirators did what they did out of envy, except for him. He was the only one who thought his actions were for the common good to his country. He lived a gentle life, so that Nature would say, "That was a man!"

Let's honor his life and put his body in my tent. Call the field to rest and let's go away to celebrate this happy day.

Most like a soldier, order'd honorably.—
So, call the field to rest; and let's away,
To part the glories of this happy day.

Exit.

THE END

Made in the USA
Columbia, SC
18 September 2019